HOW TO LIVE HEROICALLY

A Note on Translation

The passages of the *Odyssey* included in this volume were originally translated by the classicist Augustus Taber Murray and first published in 1919. Any amendments I have made are indicated through the use of [square brackets].

DR. JEAN MENZIES

HOW TO LIVE HEROICALLY

Timeless Wisdom from Homer's *Odyssey*

ILLUSTRATIONS BY BÁRBARA MALAGOLI

RIZZOLI UNIVERSE

Contents

INTRODUCTION

There is something a little surreal in sitting down to write a book inspired by Homer's *Odyssey*. In those words alone, you have two of the most recognizable names of antiquity; names you have likely imbibed, whether intentionally or not. After all, Homer's *Odyssey* is all around us: in literature, film, theater, and beyond. Even the word "odyssey" has become synonymous with long and eventful journeys. You might have used it yourself once or twice. Yet it originally spoke of one very specific journey: that of Odysseus. For that is all "odyssey" means in Ancient Greek—the story of Odysseus. Straightforward and to the point as any book title has ever been.

Or is it? Because in reality the *Odyssey* is more than just the story of Odysseus. It is the tale of Telemachus, his son, Penelope, his wife, as well as countless other figures from the mythology of ancient Greece, both divine and mortal. For millennia, ordinary people such as ourselves have seen themselves reflected in these stories and characters. Through the successes and failures of these figures we have learned lessons and found comfort in the parallels we see with our own experiences.

A single poem it may be, yet the *Odyssey* manages to touch on countless themes and ideas; many of which I explore in this volume. From the ancient Greek concept of *xenia,* or hospitality, and what that might look like today, to why you should cry sometimes; from the importance of remembering the past, to the value of literature and the arts. Many of the narrative episodes within the *Odyssey* read like allegories, deliberately designed to offer commentary on human nature and how we ought to behave. Whether it is the Lotus Eaters speaking

of the risks of temptation, or the incident with the Cyclops and what it tells us about the danger of pride. With such a wealth of material to work with, is it any wonder we continue to rewrite, retell, and reimagine a story composed millennia ago? For one of the most enduring aspects of the *Odyssey* is the timeless nature of many of these lessons. Lessons we continue to connect to through the millennia. And just as the *Odyssey* imparts meaning through its pages, so we are able to bring meaning to the words as we read them. That is the long tradition to which this book belongs.

Who is Homer and what is the *Odyssey*?

Dating from around the eighth or seventh century BCE, the *Odyssey* is an ancient Greek epic poem. By this I mean it is a long narrative written in verse. Prior to the third century BCE, it was almost unheard of for stories to be told in prose as we are used to in the modern novel. It also means that as I write this book in 2025, the *Odyssey* is almost 3,000 years old. Though we have lost many ancient texts to the ravages of time, the *Odyssey* has survived, thanks to its continued transmission down through the centuries. Impressive right? The *Odyssey* is certainly not the oldest piece of literature in existence, but it does hold second place in the European canon. In fact, it is generally accepted that the only surviving work to predate the *Odyssey* is the *Iliad*, also attributed to Homer.

But who exactly was Homer? Well, the problem is we really don't know. Though in ancient sources he is often referred to as a blind poet from Chios, none of these sources are contemporary with the *Iliad* or *Odyssey* themselves. Thus, the question of Homer's true identity has plagued classical scholars for centuries, if not longer. In fact, it would take more time to read all the various debates on the subject than it would the *Odyssey* twice over. For now, it is worth knowing that there are two main theories argued for and against. One is that Homer was a singular man and composer. This is how he is referred to by later ancient sources, but, as I mentioned, none of these sources are contemporary with Homer himself. The other theory is that the name "Homer" reflects the efforts of multiple writers, all of whom contributed to the composition of the *Odyssey*. This theory stems in part from the fact that the *Odyssey* features multiple ancient Greek dialects rather than just one. Moreover, the question of if this was the same man or a group that wrote the *Iliad* is also hotly debated.

Whether you lean toward there being one author or many when reading the *Odyssey*, the collaborative nature of the poem is undeniable. The tale of Odysseus was by no means a Homeric invention. Rather, the *Odyssey* takes on the task of recounting mythical stories that already existed; featuring gods and heroes that no singular person can be given credit for inventing. Prior to the era in which the *Odyssey* was composed, these stories would have largely been shared orally. Between the twelfth and eighth centuries BCE, the portion of the Mediterranean we now think of as ancient Greece was essentially illiterate. Instead, idealized tales of the earlier Bronze Age were recited by individuals for audiences large and small. The influences of oral tradition are also evident in the

Odyssey itself. For example, Homer (whoever he is/they are) frequently uses epithets for characters—descriptive phrases such as "bright-eyed Athena" that repeatedly accompany character's names. Using these epithets helped performers to memorize the text.

Though influenced by an oral tradition, it is unlikely—if not impossible—that Homer's *Odyssey* was ever recited from memory in its entirety. Such a feat could take anywhere from twelve to twenty-four hours and, let's be honest, ancient people had other things to do with their day. We should also consider that the *Odyssey* as we read it may feature inventions of the author—or authors—that never appeared in these stories before. Just like when you tell a friend a story, then they pass it on but a few of the details change or disappear, this is equally true of oral poetry and mythology more broadly. Thus, supposing a man named Homer did decide to write down a version of Odysseus' story, possibly for the first time, he may very well have remembered things differently from another poet when they do the same. He might also have consciously added or changed details as he saw fit. In the same vein, when you read any ancient Greek myth, you are almost guaranteed to find a different version recorded by someone else.

So, Homer—the idea—certainly deserves some credit for the *Odyssey*. And Homer very much is an idea. We may never know for sure if Homer was one man or a representative of many, but we do know that he was as revered by later generations of ancient Greeks as he is today. The fifth-century-BCE Athenian historian Thucydides, for example, quotes a hymn in honor of the god Apollo, which describes Homer as the "sweetest singer" (ἥδιστος ἀοιδῶν). And it's not just Thucydides. Homer is praised by philosophers and historians, poets, and orators alike, demonstrating that the idea of Homer at least is an influential one. This is the Homer I will be referring to throughout this book.

To return to the *Odyssey* itself, it is worth digging a little deeper into its contents for those who might not have read it recently, or at all. I have written this book both for those who know the text well and are seeking new meanings from it, and those who are looking for an entry point into this legendary work. The text of the *Odyssey* is divided into twenty-four books—essentially chapters for modern readers—though these divisions were very likely created by later ancient scholars transcribing the work. These twenty-four books cover the final thirty to forty days of Odysseus' journey and return to Ithaca after the Trojan War. In total, however, the hero has spent almost a decade at sea, fighting to get back home, and we hear of the various obstacles he has faced prior to this through flashbacks.

Through these flashbacks and recollections, we also learn a little of the Trojan War from which Odysseus is returning. Particularly from the mouths of those who fought alongside him and are equally affected by it. In some ways, you learn more details regarding the war fought between the Greeks and the Trojans in the *Odyssey* than the *Iliad*. Although the latter is often viewed as the "prequel" to the *Odyssey*, it too is only set over a handful of days, specifically those leading up to and following the death of the Greek hero Achilles. The Illiad doesn't even mention the Trojan horse that ends it all! The *Odyssey* does though.

The ghost of the Trojan War hangs over the *Odyssey*. It is the precursor to Odysseus' journey home. For context, the war was fought at Troy between the Trojans and the Greeks, known then as the Achaeans, and lasted for a period of ten years. Ten years to add to Odysseus' time away from Ithaca. It began when Paris, son of the Trojan king Priam, either abducted or seduced Helen, the wife of the Spartan king Menelaus. Menelaus' brother Agamemnon then led the Greek expedition against Troy, bringing together various Greek kings and their armies—including Odysseus. Some might have considered the situation preordained, given that once upon a time these same kings had sworn an oath to protect Menelaus' marriage to Helen. In the end, the Greeks triumphed, though many of their number are lost, and Helen is returned to Sparta.

Thus, after a decade of war that took him away from his wife and family—a war he never wanted to join—Odysseus begins his journey home, never expecting it to last a further ten years.

However, as I have already mentioned, the *Odyssey* isn't simply the story of Odysseus either—even if that's what the title suggests. While our hero sails the seas, we also follow his wife Penelope as she fends off countless noblemen desperate to marry her (and acquire her wealth); and we join his son Telemachus as he sets out on his own mini quest to learn what he can of his father's disappearance. Just as Odysseus knows nothing of what has happened in Ithaca since he left, neither Penelope or Telemachus know for sure whether Odysseus is alive or dead. After all, between the Trojan War and Odysseus' subsequent adventures, it has been almost twenty years since the hero first left home.

Through these three main narratives and those of the other characters we meet, the *Odyssey* is packed full of stories that explore hope, grief, rage, fear, and joy. It is a positive smorgasbord of human emotions and experiences. It is only natural, therefore, that we might see ourselves reflected in its pages—ancient or not.

The *Odyssey* then and now

Now, while the premise of this book is "how to live heroically"—drawing on the various life lessons we might take away from Homer's *Odyssey*—I do think it is important to address the fact that this an ancient poem. While ancient Greece was a fountain of art and innovation, much of which we still enjoy today, it was not a utopia, nor should we romanticize ancient society. Laws and social mores varied somewhat from city-state to city-state yet there was nowhere where everyone could truly be considered equal. At its core, ancient Greece was a patriarchal civilization, built upon slavery. This is not to place the modern world on some sort of pedestal in comparison, but only to note that while there are many wonderful things we can learn from the past, we must also be willing to learn from its mistakes.

This is important to remember when discussing the *Odyssey* in any context, but particularly this one. We are not aiming to recreate the Bronze Age (when the poem is set) or archaic Greece (when it was written) but rather to consider how the words in front of us might be relevant to us today. For example, I have not included among the lessons you are about to read, "respect the gods." Of course I haven't, because, and let's be honest, most of you reading this book do not worship the ancient Greek gods; many won't be religious at all. Yet, I have to acknowledge that this is likely something an ancient reader would have taken away from Homer's work.

Nevertheless, there are countless lessons within the pages of the *Odyssey* that remain relevant regardless of your faith, or the century in which you read it. That much is undeniable. Timeless advice that might be exactly what you need to hear on a given day or week. Enough to fill an entire book in fact. Some of these lessons might seem more obvious, while others might surprise you. Living heroically is not all fighting battles and slaying monsters, believe you me.

Finding ways to contextualize this advice for modern readers, meanwhile, is simply part of a long tradition in reading and interpreting Homer's epic. This is what the first-century-BCE Roman orator Cicero did when he quoted Homer repeatedly in his philosophical writings; it is also what writers and directors Ethan and Joel Cohen did when they transported the *Odyssey* to 1930s Mississippi in their 2000 comedy-drama movie *O Brother, Where Art Thou?*

Didn't I say the *Odyssey* is all around you? From Dante's critique of Odysseus as a leader in his fourteenth-century *Inferno*, to Turner's celebration of Odysseus' cunning in his nineteenth-century oil painting *Odysseus Deriding Polyphemus*, and even *The Simpsons*' satirical take on the heroic journey in an episode from Season Thirteen of the animated show called "Tales from the Public Domain." For millennia now, we have proven ourselves to be endlessly fascinated by the tale of Odysseus, and even this ancient historian can recognize that this is not just because we want to learn about the past. We are equally in search of a vehicle through which to understand ourselves and the world around us. Even these few examples to which I've called your attention demonstrate that there are numerous ways to adapt Homer's *Odyssey*. It only makes sense, therefore, that there might be multiple ways to interpret the poem as well. This has always been the power of art, whatever form it takes.

Really, it's impressive to think that almost 3,000 years later humans are still reading, enjoying, and learning from the same poem. The *Odyssey* is truly a narrative that belongs to everyone, with each new reader finding and bringing new meaning to the text. So, while you are reading this book—whether this is from cover to cover or dipping in and out—remember that we are constantly in conversation with the original poem. These lessons will teach you a little about ancient Greece and the ideals preserved in Homer's *Odyssey*. They will offer you possible interpretations of the mythical events as they unfold in a way that is helpful for modern readers—reminders that you are not alone nor are your feelings unusual. Finally, these lessons should leave you with some food for thought regarding how you might engage with the past in the present. All of which will hopefully help you on your personal odysseys.

THE BOOKS
of the *Odyssey*

As mentioned previously, the *Odyssey* as we read it today is split into twenty-four "books." The summaries of each of the books given here are designed to offer an overview of the poem's overall structure, to help you navigate your way through.

1.

The gods meet to discuss Odysseus' struggles and decide to help him. In disguise Athena goes to Telemachus, the son of Odysseus and Penelope, to offer him support.

2.

Telemachus tries unsuccessfully to stand up to his mother's suitors, and we also learn how Penelope has tricked them into waiting years for her answer. Telemachus then plans to make his own journey and see what he can learn of Odysseus.

3.

Telemachus visits King Nestor of Pylos and learns more about the events of the Trojan War. He is then joined by Nestor's son Peisistratus for the next leg of his journey.

4.

Telemachus arrives in Sparta and is greeted warmly by Menelaus and Helen. He is told further stories of his father's intelligence and bravery in Troy by his hosts.

5.

We finally meet Odysseus who is stranded on the island home of the nymph Calypso. Hermes is sent by the other gods to insist Calypso help Odysseus return home. Unfortunately, Odysseus' raft is sabotaged by Poseidon, and he must further rely on the gods to get him to dry land.

6.

Odysseus finds himself washed up on the coast of Phaeacia where he meets the princess Nausicaa. Nausicaa helps Odysseus and tells him how to win over her parents.

7.

Nausicaa returns home. Odysseus is then led by Athena to the king and queen of Phaeacia, Alcinous and Arete, who welcome him to their kingdom. He does not, however, reveal his identity.

8.

Odysseus and the rest of the Phaeacian court are entertained by a bard who sings songs of the Trojan War. Listening to his own memories leads Odysseus to recollect his lost friends.

9.

Odysseus takes over from the Phaeacian bard and shares his story with the king and queen. We hear about his encounter with the Lotus Eaters and the Cyclopes, including his escape from the Cyclops Polyphemus.

10.

Odysseus' recollections continue. He narrates his arrival on Circe's island, how the goddess transformed his crew into pigs, and how he won her over to his side with the help of the god Hermes.

11.

Odysseus tells the tale of how he traveled to the Underworld and spoke to various souls, including his mother and the seer Tiresias.

12.

Odysseus relates how he and his men managed to survive their encounters with first the sirens and then the monsters Scylla and Charybdis, only for him to lose them all at the hands of Zeus. This is the point in his story where he finds himself shipwrecked on the island of Calypso. Thus, we have come full circle.

13.

Odysseus leaves Phaeacia and returns to Ithaca. He meets Athena on the shore, and she uses her divine powers to disguise him as a beggar.

14.

Odysseus visits the swineherd Eumaeus in the disguise to learn what has happened in his absence. Eumaeus meanwhile impresses Odysseus with his hospitality and loyalty to his absent master.

15.

Athena informs Telemachus that it is time to return home, and he sails back to Ithaca. When he arrives, he heads straight for Eumaeus' farm where he meets the beggar.

16.

Athena tells Odysseus he should reveal his true identity to Telemachus and temporarily removes his disguise. Father and son are reunited and begin plotting the suitors' downfall.

17.

Telemachus returns to the palace alone, while Eumaeus brings the beggar (Odysseus) separately. Odysseus, still in disguise, meets the suitors and is abused by the one called Antinous.

18.

Antinous encourages another beggar named Irus to fight Odysseus for his entertainment; naturally Odysseus wins. Meanwhile, Athena sends Penelope to speak with the suitors, and the queen demands they bring her gifts if they wish to marry her.

19.

While the suitors sleep, Odysseus and Telemachus hide their weapons. Penelope speaks with the beggar (Odysseus) who tells her he once knew her husband. She then instructs Odysseus' old nurse, Eurycleia, to bathe the stranger. This is when the older woman recognizes her master from a scar on his leg.

20.

Both Odysseus and Penelope lie awake. The former worries over his chances against so many men, while the latter ponders if death would be better than having to take a husband other than Odysseus.

21.

Penelope tells the suitors that she will marry whoever can string and shoot Odysseus' infamous bow. All of them fail until Odysseus, still disguised as a beggar, takes up the challenge. He succeeds.

22.

Odysseus, now armed with his bow, shoots Antinous. He then reveals his identity to the suitors who beg for his forgiveness. Odysseus does not forgive them, however, and all are slaughtered by the king and his son.

23.

Eurycleia, having helped clean up the bloody aftermath of the slaughter, informs Penelope that Odysseus has returned. Penelope refuses to believe it is so without proof, so tests Odysseus. Odysseus passes her test and the two are reunited.

24.

Hermes escorts the souls of the suitors to the Underworld. Odysseus visits his father. Ithaca, meanwhile, learns of the suitors' deaths and their families gather to demand revenge. Before the fighting can escalate, however, Athena comes to Earth to tell them it is time for the violence to end. Ithaca is finally at peace.

THE CHARACTERS
of the *Odyssey*

The key characters of the *Odyssey* each has something to teach us. Interspersed throughout the book you will find further explorations of these characters and the role they play within the poem. You will also find profiles on three of the central locations in the poem—Troy (p. 24), the Underworld (p. 168), and Ithaca (p. 260).

Argos (p. 184)

The hunting dog whom Odysseus reared as a puppy. He still remembers his old master two decades on and, unlike everyone else, recognizes him straight away.

Athena (p. 38)

The goddess of wisdom, war, and weaving. She admires Odysseus' cunning mind and therefore champions him among the gods. She also acts as a mentor to both Odysseus and his son Telemachus throughout the epic.

Calypso (p. 88)

A nymph who resides on the island of Ogygia. She begins a romantic relationship with Odysseus when he is shipwrecked on her shores, but cannot accept his decision to return home. She refuses to let the hero leave until the gods force her.

Circe (p. 130)

A goddess renowned for her skills in magic. When Odysseus arrives on her island home of Aeaea she turns his crew into pigs. He is able to win her over with the help of Hermes, however, and she assists them all on their journey.

Eumaeus and Eurycleia (p. 154)

Two slaves in the household of Odysseus who have served him since he was a child. Eumaeus is a middle-aged man who works as a swineherd, while Eurycleia is an elderly woman who served as wet-nurse to both Odysseus and Telemachus.

Helen (p. 80)

The queen of Sparta and the wife of Menelaus. Her abduction by the Trojan prince Paris initiates the war between the Greeks and Trojans. In the *Odyssey* she has returned to Sparta and welcomes Telemachus into her and Menelaus' home.

Hermes (p. 246)

The messenger god who is usually responsible for passing on and enacting the decisions made by the council of gods on Olympus. He appears on multiple occasions throughout the *Odyssey* to assist Odysseus.

Menelaus (p. 176)

The king of Sparta and the husband of Helen. He led the Greeks in the Trojan War alongside his brother Agamemnon in order to retrieve Helen. In the *Odyssey* he has returned home safely and acts as an enthusiastic host to Telemachus.

Nausicaa (p. 114)

A princess from the island of Phaeacia, Nausicaa is the daughter of King Alcinous and Queen Arete. She finds Odysseus washed up on her shores and helps him in his time of need. Though the possibility of her marrying Odysseus is raised, as we know, Odysseus is already married.

Nestor (p. 72)

The king of Pylos and the oldest among the Greek kings who fought at Troy. He is renowned for his wisdom, and is therefore the first person Telemachus visits when seeking information regarding his father.

Odysseus (p. 220)

The king of Ithaca and the central character of Homer's *Odyssey*. He is married to Penelope with whom he has one son, Telemachus. Twenty years prior to the events of the epic he left to fight in the Trojan War. After the ten-year war was over, however, it took him another decade to find his way home.

Penelope (p. 238)

The queen of Ithaca and the wife of Odysseus. She is also the mother of Telemachus. She has not seen her husband in almost two decades but refuses to take another husband despite her various suitors. She is praised for her intellect and loyalty.

Polyphemus (p. 122)

The son of Poseidon. He is a species of one-eyed giant in Greek mythology known as a Cyclops. He lives on an island inhabited by other Cyclopes, where he herds sheep. He also has a taste for human flesh and threatens to eat Odysseus and his men.

Poseidon (p. 106)

The god of the sea and brother of Zeus. Poseidon is one of Odysseus' primary obstacles in the *Odyssey*, using his power over the waters to delay his journey after the hero blinds his son Polyphemus.

Scylla and Charybdis (p. 146)

Two mythical monsters who reside on opposite sides of the Strait of Messina through which Odysseus must sail with his crews. Scylla is described as a many-headed monster who eats passers-by, while Charybdis is an unidentifiable creature who creates whirlpools that swallow ships.

The Suitors (p. 46)

A group of noblemen from Ithaca and the surrounding islands. They were too young to fight at Troy and are now looking to increase their wealth and power through a marriage to Penelope. They are characterized as greedy, violent, and arrogant throughout the *Odyssey*.

Telemachus (p. 54)

The son of Odysseus and Penelope. He was but a baby when his father left for Troy and thus only knows him through the stories of others. He starts off the epic with little experience but gradually grows into a confident young man.

Tiresias (p. 138)

A now deceased seer; unlike the other souls of the dead, he has retained his knowledge and reason. He is visited by Odysseus in the Underworld, so that he might instruct the hero on how to return home.

Zeus (p. 212)

The god of justice, hospitality, and thunder; he also rules over the other gods from Mount Olympus. In the *Odyssey* he acts as arbitrator among the gods and gives Athena permission to help Odysseus.

TROY

Understanding where we came from

Troy, also known as Ilion, was a kingdom located to the east of the Mediterranean, in Asia Minor (modern-day Turkey). It was also a very real place, so we must be cautious of blurring the line between Troy, the historical site, and Troy, the mythological kingdom. It is, of course, the latter which is the subject of this book.

In the time of Odysseus, the mythological Troy was ruled by King Priam and Queen Hecuba. Together they had quite the cohort of children, but the one name that's most relevant to the events that unfold next is Paris. Born Alexandros, Paris was the subject of a prophetic dream that told his parents he would be the downfall of Troy. Unable to kill their newborn baby, however, they sent the herdsman Agelaus to do the job. Agelaus, however, kept the child and raised him as his own, using the name Paris.

Meanwhile on Olympus, a bitter debate had arisen among three goddesses: Aphrodite, Athena, and Hera. The question? Who was the most beautiful. When they could not decide among themselves, they went to Zeus for help. The king of the gods then appointed the mortal Paris as their judge. Each goddess offered Paris a different prize should he pick her, but it was Aphrodite's offer of Helen's hand in marriage that Paris chose. A choice that, ultimately, led to the Trojan War.

→

The [bard], moved by the god, began, and let his song be heard, taking up the tale where the Argives had embarked on their benched ships and were sailing away, after throwing fire on their huts, while those others led by glorious Odysseus were now [sitting in the Trojan assembly place], hidden in the horse. 8.499–504

To discuss Troy in the context of Homer's *Odyssey* is to discuss the Trojan War. When Paris—who had since been recognized as Priam's son—returned to Troy with Helen, Greece followed. Menelaus, Agamemnon, Odysseus, Ajax, and Achilles, the strongest and most capable Greek heroes, led an army of thousands to retrieve Menelaus' wife. A task that would take them ten whole years.

When we meet Odysseus, therefore, he is a veteran returning home from war. A war in which he witnessed the deaths of countless men, both friend and foe. The Greeks may have won, but they did not all survive. Those who did, meanwhile, leave Troy with the weight of what they experienced heavy on their shoulders. They are not the same men who left home a decade earlier, Odysseus included.

Unsurprisingly, the Greek's victory in Troy is celebrated by a number of the characters we meet during the *Odyssey*; figures from far and wide sing the praises of the glorious heroes who fought on the winning side. There is an air of idealism, particularly among those who were not there. This is not so for Odysseus and his friends.

When Odysseus listens to a Phaeacian bard recount the defeat of the Trojans, he is overwhelmed with grief and brought to tears. When Menelaus recounts his time in Troy to Telemachus, he declares he would give up the wealth he won should his comrades' lives be returned to them. And when Odysseus meets Achilles in the Underworld, the hero informs him it is better to be alive and ordinary than die in glory as he chose.

The Odyssey *is not a book about glory. It is a book about a man who simply wants his family back. Troy is the first stop along this journey, but it is certainly not where it ends.*

It is also worth remembering that Odysseus never actually wanted to go to Troy. He would much rather have remained in Ithaca, beside his wife and son, ruling over his people. But sometimes life takes us to places we would rather not go. Whether it's due to a promise we have made, as Odysseus had done, or simply because our circumstances demand it and there's no other way. As Odysseus goes to Troy and is changed by it, sometimes it is necessary to accept the path ahead, and see what we can take from it.

The *Odyssey* is not a book about glory. It is a book about a man who simply wants his family back. Troy is the first stop along this journey, but it is certainly not where it ends. This is an important perspective for us all to take. Life will often lead us down unexpected roads or hand us difficult circumstances, but these do not mark the end of our voyage. The experiences we've had will shape us, certainly, as Odysseus and his men's lives are forever changed by their time in Troy. But they don't have to define us. We can choose where we travel next. The *Odyssey* reminds us that while it's important to look back, and to understand where we have come from, we must ultimately look to the future and continue on our journey.

Tell me, Muse, of [a wily] man, driven far astray after he had sacked the sacred citadel of Troy. Many were the men whose cities he saw and whose minds he learned, and many the woes he suffered in his heart upon the sea, seeking to win his own life and the return of his comrades. Yet even so he did not save his comrades, for all his desire, for through their own blind folly they perished—fools, who devoured the cattle of Helios Hyperion; whereupon he took from them the day of their returning. Of these things, goddess, daughter of Zeus, beginning where you will, tell us in our turn.

Now all the rest, as many as had escaped sheer destruction, were at home, safe from both war and sea; but that man alone, filled with longing for his return and for his wife, did the queenly nymph Calypso, that beautiful goddess, keep prisoner in her hollow caves, yearning that he should be her husband. But when, as the seasons revolved, the year came in which the gods had ordained that he should return home to Ithaca, not even then was he free from toils and among his own people. And all the gods pitied him except Poseidon; he continued to rage unceasingly against godlike Odysseus until at length he reached his own land.

But now Poseidon had gone among the far-off Ethiopians—the Ethiopians who dwell divided in two, the farthermost of men, some where Hyperion sets and some where he rises—there to receive a hecatomb [an ancient Greek sacrifice] of bulls and rams, and there he was taking his joy, sitting at the feast; but the other gods were gathered together in the halls of Olympian Zeus. Among them the father of gods and men was the first to speak, for in his heart he thought of flawless Aegisthus, whom far-famed Orestes, Agamemnon's son, had slain.

1.1–31

LESSON ONE

INSPIRATION IS THE FIRST STEP

Tell me, Muse, of [a wily] man, driven far astray
after he had sacked the sacred citadel of Troy.

1.1–2

What better way to start our journey through the life lessons in Homer's *Odyssey* than at the very beginning, the moment when Homer calls on the Muse to tell him a story, to inspire him. For this is the role of the muses. To assist us mere mortals in the creation of art.

In Homer's time there was no standard number of muses, whose roles varied from region to region. Today, however, we often remember the nine muses whose names were standardized during the Classical period. These muses were: Calliope, of epic poetry; Clio, of history; Polymnia, of sacred poetry; Euterpe, of lyric poetry; Erato, of erotic poetry; Melpomene, of tragedy; Thalia, of comedy; Ourania, of astronomy; and Terpsichore, of music.

Naturally, many have been eager to assume that Homer, therefore, calls to Calliope when he addresses the Muse in his poetry. Without any pre-Classical evidence to support these roles, however, it is an impossible claim to verify. Nor does it entirely matter in the context we are discussing them for it is enough to know that the muses, including Homer's Muse, are goddesses of inspiration.

This is also one of the few moments when Homer, whoever that is, breaks the fourth wall as it were. We hear directly from the poet regarding his hopes and intentions. His desire to tell a truly epic story. In giving us this window into his process, we are also able to relate to the poem's composer(s) despite knowing little to nothing about who they really are. Because they're just like us: looking for inspiration.

Homer isn't exactly attempting a small feat either. The poet seeks to tell the tale of an already legendary figure. Odysseus' story is a complex one with so many moving parts it can sometimes be hard to keep track. It features gods and goddesses, monsters and mortals, all the while capturing the length and breadth of real human emotion.

I cannot claim to truly know anything of the *Odyssey*'s writing process, besides that which I outlined in the introduction. Did its composer or composers worry over their capability or doubt their skills? Who knows. They certainly didn't need to, but when has that ever stopped anyone? What I will say, however, is that while we should commend Homer for the resulting output, we might also thank him (or them) for reminding us that we all start somewhere. We start by looking for inspiration.

This is the role of the muses.
To assist us mere mortals
in the creation of art.

LESSON TWO

TAKE RESPONSIBILITY

"It's astonishing how ready mortals are to blame the gods. It is from us, they say, that evils come, but they even by themselves, through their own blind folly, have sorrows beyond that which is ordained."

1.32–34

One might anticipate that in a world ruled over by gods and goddesses free will is in limited supply. According to Greek mythology, however, things are far more complex than simply blaming the Olympians for all your woes.

When you crack open the spine on the *Odyssey*, you are greeted not by a scene of Odysseus at sea or his son and wife in Ithaca, but one of Zeus and Athena in conversation on Mount Olympus. Rather than the poem's protagonists, we are first introduced to those all-powerful observers of mortal lives. For the gods are not in charge. They can offer good advice, punish those who have angered them, and even offer companionship along the way. What they cannot do is determine the outcome of the story—that is in the hands of its mortal heroes.

This is what Zeus tells us anyway. As he and his daughter discuss the fate of the titular Odysseus, the god observes that it is a tendency among humans to blame their deities for all the evil that befalls them. Yet Zeus points out that more often than not their circumstances are a result of their own decisions. As an example, he highlights the case of Aegisthus.

→

Aegisthus made the choice to bed the already married Clytemnestra while her husband Agamemnon was away at war. He then proceeded to kill the other man upon his return and install himself as king of his household. And what does Aegisthus receive in return for his actions? He is eventually slain by Agamemnon's son Orestes. None of Aegisthus' actions were preordained by the gods. He was not simply the victim of destiny. He had other choices, yet this was the path he took.

This is not to say that life is sometimes outside of our control. According to Homer, all humans are guaranteed a certain amount of pain in life. Think of this as the inevitable trials of life, the accidents, the inequalities outside of our control. Anything beyond this, however, is brought on by humans themselves. Life, therefore, is a mix of fate and choices.

Zeus accepts responsibility for the former and thus he cannot fathom why mortals cannot own up to the latter. It is not he who set Aegisthus on his path to self-destruction, however much the man might like to blame him. His suffering is far "beyond that which is ordained," as Zeus puts it. Elsewhere in the *Odyssey* it is also up to the heroes to listen to the gods and goddesses who advise them; their hand is never forced one way or the other.

Zeus' words meanwhile may as well be written explicitly for Homer's readers. Do not try to pass the blame when your actions have unpleasant consequences. Take responsibility for what you yourself have control over.

Life is a mix
of fate
and choices.

ATHENA

It is too simple to refer to Athena as the "goddess of war and wisdom," yet this is all too often how we are first introduced to her in popular culture. She is a striking figure wearing a mixture of women's dress and the kind of armor more often associated with men in antiquity. She stands alongside the most powerful Olympian gods, the strategic counterpart to the war god Ares' brawn. There is an element of truth to these ideas, of course, but it is also a relatively one-dimensional vision of an incredibly complex figure—a figure who is integral to the events of the *Odyssey*. She is the story's guiding light, if you will, with many characteristics worth emulating. In the quote below we see her advocating for her mentee, Odysseus; her leadership when dealing with other gods; and her willingness to take action to achieve her ends.

Homer's Athena is a friend and advisor. She is known as Athena Xenia—goddess of hospitality; Pallas Athena—the young girl; Athena Glaukopis—bright-eyed Athena, an epithet that nods to her intelligence; and Athena, daughter of Zeus—a descriptor that is pretty self-explanatory, but you should never underestimate the magnitude of being the child of the king of the gods himself.

From the moment she is born, Athena is a powerful player in the games of gods and mortals; even her birth is a rather interesting tale. Zeus, as the story goes, slept with the goddess Metis—a goddess of wisdom from the previous generation of deities known as the Titans. Unfortunately for Metis a prophesy declared that any son born of the goddess would be

→

Then the goddess, [bright-eyed] Athene, answered him: "Father of us all, son of Cronus, high above all lords, if indeed this is now well-pleasing to the blessed gods, that the wise Odysseus should return to his own home, let us send forth Hermes, the guide, Argeïphontes, to the isle Ogygia, that with all speed he may declare to the fair-tressed nymph our fixed resolve, namely the return of steadfast Odysseus, that he may come home. But, as for me, I will go to Ithaca, that I may the more arouse his son, and set courage in his heart." 1.80–89

more powerful than his father. Terrified he might be overthrown by his son, Zeus literally swallowed Metis. After some time had passed, however, Zeus was overwhelmed with an excruciating headache. Desperate to be free of the pain, he asked his fellow gods to strike his head with an axe; from the gash Athena was born fully formed. In this way, she is truly her father's daughter. Yet, she also encapsulates many of her mother's best qualities, as a goddess of good council and crafts. Affinities she wields throughout the *Odyssey*.

There are therefore too many other myths in which Athena features to unpack them all here. Yet, in the *Odyssey* alone, we witness many of the qualities that made her a figure to be both loved and feared in antiquity, and that we can easily admire today. Throughout Homer's poem she wears a great many hats, taking on the form of mortals, dreams, and even herself to ease the paths of its heroes with her knowledge and experience. In truth, the *Odyssey* would be nothing without her.

Before we meet Odysseus, Telemachus, or Penelope, we meet Athena. She and the other gods are gathered on Mount Olympus to discuss the fate of our unlucky hero. It is Athena, above all others, who champions this mortal man. Athena is never afraid to take an active role in the narrative of the *Odyssey* or the lives of those she cares about. Her first act in the *Odyssey* is to advocate for Odysseus and his family among the other gods. She sees in him a little of her own cunning intelligence and insists that the gods step in to help him when he is trapped on Calypso's Island. Meanwhile, she vows to take on various human disguises in order to assist Odysseus and his family.

Thus, Athena's second act is to visit Telemachus in person and instill in him renewed courage in the face of endless misery. This is one of the ways in which her roles as goddess of war and wisdom come together in the *Odyssey*. With her strength of conviction, she is able to rouse others to action, just as she does herself.

Equally as important is the fact that Athena also knows when to step back and let those she cares about own the decisions they make. She lends a helping hand throughout the *Odyssey*, offering both guidance and encouragement where she can, but in the end, she leaves things in the hands of the individual. It is up to them if they want to follow her good advice.

Of course, all of this makes Athena an equally powerful foe, and a capricious one at that. Athena, like most ancient Greek gods and goddesses, can be both violent and vindictive. It is not for nothing she is often dubbed "terrible" Athena in the ancient texts. When she hates you, she really hates you. Yet, when she loves you, she loves you fiercely and the benefits of this are perfectly encapsulated within the *Odyssey*.

You do not need to be a goddess or even under the patronage of one to take something away from Athena's role in the *Odyssey*. She is committed to the people she cares about. She does not waver when things are difficult. She is willing to share her wisdom and lend a helping hand. She does not strong-arm or take over for others but rather leaves the choice in their hands. She stands up for what she believes in, among her peers, and when faced with those more powerful than her. Nor can she be defined by one thing; she is complex and multifaceted (she's also the goddess of weaving, don't you know?). Whether in the role of mentor, friend, or partner, channeling these qualities from Athena would make you an excellent support to those around you.

She is known as Athena Xenia—goddess of hospitality; Pallas Athena—the young girl; Athena Glaukopis—bright-eyed Athena, an epithet that nods to her intelligence; and Athena, daughter of Zeus

LESSON THREE

LET GO OF YOUR ANGER

"But come, let [those of] us who are here all
give thought to his return, how he may come home;
and Poseidon will let go his anger, for he will in
no way be able, against all the immortal gods
and in their despite, to contend alone."

1.75–79

If it were not for the mighty god of the sea Poseidon, Odysseus might have made it home far, far sooner than he did. Throughout the *Odyssey*, the god regularly stirs up the waters and sends storms from above to delay the hero's journey. Really, it's no wonder it took Odysseus ten years to get home. What could possibly make one god so angry? Well, while Poseidon's animosity runs deep, there is one major incident which incites his ire and that is the blinding of his son: Polyphemus.

During the early stages of his voyage home, Odysseus and his crew moor their ship upon the island of the Cyclopes—a race of one-eyed giants in Greek mythology. While the rest of his companions await them, Odysseus and a small band of men head inland to the cave of Polyphemus. When Polyphemus discovers them, however, he is far from amenable to guests and promptly eats two of Odysseus' men before trapping them in the cave.

Of course, Odysseus devises an escape plan, one that involves a burning stake being pushed into the single eye socket of the Cyclops—hence Poseidon's wrath.

Now, I think it is important to acknowledge that anger is a perfectly natural emotion, just like sadness or joy. There is a place for anger and denying its validity doesn't get us anywhere. Anger can be an understandable and appropriate response in certain situations. We can probably all appreciate here why Poseidon was upset in the first place. Anger can even be useful or cathartic. Yet there comes a point when no matter the circumstances anger ceases to serve us—at least this is what Zeus means when he suggests it is time for Poseidon to "let go his anger."

In many ways Poseidon is positioned in opposition not just to Odysseus, a mortal, but also to the rest of the gods and the goddesses throughout the *Odyssey*. When the time comes for Odysseus to return home, Athena, Zeus, and the other gods come together to support the hero in the final stages of his journey. All but Poseidon. The god does not deny Odysseus will make it home; he cannot go entirely against the will of Zeus. But he certainly won't make it easy.

This is exactly Zeus' point. In the end, Poseidon's ire will prove futile: "He will in no way be able, against all the immortal gods ... to contend alone." Odysseus will return home. It is his destiny. Poseidon cannot change this fate any more than we can change the color of the sky. Meanwhile, if we allow our anger to destroy everything in its wake, there will eventually be nothing left. While it can be useful, eventually there will come a time when our anger will not serve us; when this time arrives the best decision we can make is to let it go, and move on to what comes next.

Anger can even be useful
or cathartic. Yet there comes
a point when no matter
the circumstances anger
ceases to serve us.

THE SUITORS

Arrogant, greedy, violent, cruel, and ungrateful. As a unit, the suitors may as well represent everything that you don't want to be, according to Homer. They are the closest thing the *Odyssey* has to an overarching antagonist—discounting Poseidon as he only really cares about causing harm to Odysseus. The suitors, meanwhile, sit in Odysseus' home, abuse his household, gorge themselves on his livestock, attempt to steal his wife, and even plot the murder of his son.

Generally speaking, the suitors are treated as a group throughout Homer's *Odyssey*. They are all young noblemen from Ithaca and its neighboring islands who hope to win the hand of Queen Penelope. They assume, like many, that her husband has died at sea, and arrive at Odysseus' palace shortly after the Trojan War has ended. While they vie for Penelope's hand, they set up camp in the palace itself, and refuse to leave until she has chosen one from among them. And there are a lot of them. According to Telemachus, the suitors number 108, though all 108 are never named. Still, a few names do stand out from the rest.

Antinous is one of the group's two leaders, characterized as particularly cruel and violent, abusing those he considers beneath him. Eurymachus is the second of the group's leaders, and often deemed to be Penelope's primary suitor. As a man he is depicted as clever, yet manipulative. He pretends to be a friend to both Penelope and Telemachus, while colluding in the plot to kill the young prince from the start.

→

There [Athena] found the proud suitors. They were taking their pleasure at checkers in front of the doors, sitting on the hides of oxen which they themselves had slain; and of the heralds and busy squires, some were mixing wine and water for them in bowls, others again were washing the tables with porous sponges and setting them out, while still others were portioning out meats in abundance. 1.106–12

It is significant that when we first meet the suitors it is through the lens of their ineptitude as hosts. Athena, disguised as a man named Mentor, has come to the palace to speak with Telemachus. Upon her arrival, however, she is ignored by the suitors who are playing games, drinking wine, and eating meat in excess. Telemachus, on the other hand, goes to Athena (Mentor) as soon as he sees her. Ashamed of the suitors' behavior, he welcomes her to his home, offering her a place to sit and something to eat.

The concept of *xenia,* or hospitality, was extremely important in ancient Greece, and understood to be particularly valued by Zeus, the most powerful of the gods. It is unsurprising then that in the *Odyssey* adherence to the code of *xenia* is a key way of distinguishing who is admirable and who is not. The bad behavior of the suitors is woven throughout the *Odyssey*, escalating with each book. It's impossible to catalog each misdeed. From gluttony to violence, however, they are basically the worst guests imaginable. It is not simply the fact they propose to Penelope that ensures their fate. It is the way in which they have taken advantage of Penelope, Telemachus, and the rest of Odysseus' household. Hospitality, kindness to strangers, generosity, and courtesy are all timeless values, which remain as important today as they were in Ancient Greece. With the shocking example of the suitors Homer gives us an unsubtle reminder to maintain these qualities. None of us would wish to behave like a suitor.

When our hero returns to Ithaca and learns of the suitors' actions, he immediately begins to plot their downfall. Due to their numbers Odysseus knows he must tread carefully. Disguised as a beggar he infiltrates their gathering with the help of Telemachus. No one suspects him of being the long-lost king and so they underestimate him. When Penelope introduces the contest to see who can use Odysseus' bow, he has the perfect opportunity to take them by surprise. The last to try after all the suitors have failed, he masterfully strings

Hospitality, kindness to strangers, generosity, and courtesy are all timeless values, which remain as important today as they were in Ancient Greece

the bow and shoots Antinous just as he is about to take a sip of wine. With one suitor eliminated, Odysseus reveals his identity, and the rest of the shocked suitors cower at his feet. Eurymachus, of course, attempts to bargain for the rest of their lives. He argues that Antinous was their leader and he was to blame for everything. It is an argument that gets him nowhere, and the slaughter then begins.

There is one suitor who is portrayed as more respectful of both his hosts and the gods: Amphinomus. When his cohort suggests killing Telemachus, he tries to dissuade them, only agreeing on the condition that the gods themselves condone it. We also witness him offer bread and wine to Odysseus in his beggar's disguise, while the other suitors mock him. There is even a chance that Amphinomus might survive the massacre, as Odysseus warns him the day before that if he remains, he will die. Amphinomus, however, was still one of the suitors and Athena binds him to the palace, so he cannot leave.

Amphinomus might have been slightly better, but he still worked with the group when it suited him. Sometimes, it is easier to go with the majority than to stand up for what we believe in, or for what is right. Sometimes, we may imagine our behavior is not as damaging because we're a follower rather than a leader. This could not be further from the truth. The fate of Amphinomus should remind us that following the herd isn't an excuse and will not save you from judgment.

The suitors laughed in the face of one of the most important values of the Homeric world: hospitality. They didn't just make one small mistake; they consistently proved themselves to be the opposite of the heroic Odysseus. When Odysseus learned from his pride, they doubled down. While Odysseus showed his hosts gratitude, they took more than they deserved. Whereas Odysseus tried to do right by his people, they mistreated everyone around them. Simply put: the suitors are the antithesis of everything positive the *Odyssey* hopes to teach.

LESSON FOUR

DON'T HOLD YOURSELF BACK

Wise Telemachus answered her: "Mentor, how shall I go, and how shall I greet him? I am as yet unversed in subtle speech, and moreover [it is shameful for] a young man to question an elder."

Then the goddess, [bright-eyed] Athena, answered him: "Telemachus, some things you yourself will devise in your breast, and other things heaven too will prompt you. For I do not think you were born and reared without the favor of the gods."

3.21–28

When we first meet Telemachus, he is defined by what he does not have. He does not have the power to evict his mother's unwelcome suitors from his home. He has no memories of the father who is so lauded by those around him. And he has no experience of the world beyond the island of Ithaca where he has spent the entirety of his young life thus far. This is reflected in the way he views himself. He considers his inexperience a failing and says as much to the goddess Athena while she is disguised as Mentor. Athena, on the other hand, disagrees.

What Athena tells Telemachus, and us in turn, is that inexperience is not a shortcoming; it is an opportunity. For the only way to grow, is to seek out that which you have not yet experienced. To step beyond what you know and try your hand at something new.

In many ways, Athena's words set not just Telemachus, but us as readers up for the rest of the poem. We witness Telemachus' journey in tandem with that of Odysseus. With the help of the gods, Telemachus sails away from Ithaca to visit the kingdoms of his father's friends. He meets new people. He listens to their stories. He encounters challenges and he learns what he can before returning home. And when he returns, he is no longer the inexperienced young man he declared himself in Book Three. He is a hero in his own right, ready to fight for his home alongside his father, rather than watching from the sidelines as he has done for so long.

This is Telemachus' journey, but only because he heeds Athena's advice. He does not let his inexperience hold him back; rather he embraces what the world can teach him and seeks it out with the aid of those who would help him. This is not just a journey reserved for the sons of Greek heroes, however. It is a journey we all must embark on.

So, remember, the next time you don't feel adequate or experienced enough for a situation, you are simply at the beginning. We all start somewhere. We cannot know what we do not know. The lesson is not to let that hold you back. The only way to grow is to embrace the journey; take the leap and see where you end up.

Inexperience is not
a shortcoming; it is
an opportunity.

TELEMACHUS

You might be surprised to learn that the *Odyssey* does not in fact open with the adventures of Odysseus, but his son Telemachus. Like his famous father Telemachus goes on a physical journey during the *Odyssey*, but perhaps more importantly he also experiences an emotional transformation. Telemachus' journey, therefore, offers an inspiring tale of how one young man is able to learn and grow from what life throws at him.

Telemachus is the only child of Odysseus and his wife Penelope. We first meet him as a young man, approximately twenty years old. He is strong, handsome, and a prince to boot; surely his life is a pleasant one? Unfortunately for Telemachus, his story thus far has been defined by one thing: the absence of his father. Only an infant when Odysseus left for Troy, Telemachus grew up waiting for the return of a father he never knew. In the meantime, he has witnessed a slew of unwanted suitors descend on his home to vie for his mother's hand, and drain the resources of the land he should one day rule over. All this has left its mark, and the prince we are introduced to in Book One of the *Odyssey* is actually rather a miserable one.

Telemachus in Book One of the *Odyssey* is many things. He is lost, inexperienced, confused, angry, and frustrated. He wants the suitors to leave; he wants his inheritance restored; and most of all he wants a chance to know the father he can barely remember—the father who may or may not be

→

The godlike Telemachus was far the first to see her, for he was sitting among the suitors, troubled at heart, seeing in thought his noble father ... As he thought of these things, sitting among the suitors, he beheld Athene, and he went straight to the outer door; for in his heart he counted it a shame that a stranger should stand long at the gates. 1.113–18

alive. For readers I think this makes him particularly human; particularly relatable.

Like his father, Telemachus also has the favor of the goddess Athena. Athena, who has watched over Odysseus for many years, now goes to his son and encourages Telemachus to travel across the Mediterranean in search of news regarding his father.

First, Telemachus travels to Pylos, the kingdom of Odysseus' comrade Nestor, and then to Sparta to meet King Menelaus and Queen Helen. Both Nestor and Menelaus tell Telemachus tales of Odysseus' exploits in Troy, but not of what happened to Odysseus after he left. After these meetings Athena returns to Telemachus to inform him it is time to go home.

Telemachus' travels are more than just an opportunity to tell a tale or two, however. This is Telemachus' hero's journey. The "hero's journey" is something of a rite of passage in Greek mythology. One in which the hero is initiated into the ways of adulthood—a coming of age if you will. Usually this looks like leaving home, overcoming trials, and returning home renewed. Unlike Odysseus, who journeys to find Ithaca, Telemachus journeys to find himself.

Through his journey, Telemachus gains confidence and experience, which he demonstrates upon his return to Ithaca. First, he is able to avoid the suitors' assassination attempts. He is then reunited with the father he had lost and plays an important role in his father's triumphant return, and in restoring peace. Thus, throughout the narrative of the *Odyssey*, Telemachus not only finds his father but becomes a hero in his own right.

While we might not live in Bronze Age Greece, that does not mean we do not all experience our own equivalent of Telemachus' hero quest. Whether physical or emotional, life will inevitably take us on our own journey and we will face our own challenges. Facing these challenges will help make us who we are. Telemachus physically ends up in the same place he started. The thing he thought he was looking for (Odysseus) he could have found just by waiting in Ithaca—but it is the journey that matters. What Telemachus tells us is that we grow as people by embracing the journey.

Telemachus goes on a physical journey, but also an emotional transformation throughout the *Odyssey*.

LESSON FIVE

DEATH IS A PART OF LIFE

"But clearly death, that is common to all,
not even the gods themselves can ward off,
even from a man they love, whenever the fell fate
of pitiless death strikes him down."

3.236–38

I don't want to sound defeatist, but everybody dies. In the words of Athena herself: not even the gods can prevent the inevitable loss of mortal life. It's an undeniable truth, yet it is one many of us struggle with. Whether it is our own mortality or that of those we love, death often hangs over us like an invincible enemy—one we can only deceive ourselves can be defeated.

You might think that this seems like a somewhat dour lesson to include so soon in our exploration of the *Odyssey*. It is not for nothing, however, that Athena shares this advice with Telemachus early on. Disguised as a man named Mentor, the goddess encourages the young man not to give up on his father, or his return. Have hope she tells him; Telemachus, however, is unconvinced. The gods, Athena reminds him, are on Odysseus' side. Thus, the hero stands a better chance than many at surviving his long journey home. Still, it is in this moment she laments that even the gods cannot prevent the inevitable: death.

Athena doesn't only drop in this little reminder to cause Telemachus distress. Rather, she is providing some perspective and reminding him that we only have the life we are given.

→

For death, loss, mortality, and grief are all constant themes throughout Homer's epic, just as they are features of life. During the narrative we witness deaths both natural and unnatural; we hear tales of loved ones whose lives were lost too soon; and we even travel to the Underworld itself to meet with those long departed. Parallels for which we will all experience in our time. Is it not, therefore, better to be prepared?

Athena encourages both Telemachus and the reader to acknowledge and accept these facts. In this way, we are better equipped to understand them. Denying death doesn't stop it happening;, it only makes it harder when loss does find us. Being secretive about grief doesn't make it go away; it simply allows it to rot and fester.

While the *Odyssey* never implies you should be unaffected by loss, it does encourage you to face it. You will have to if you are to read on. But nor does Homer's epic suggest you should give up on yourself or others. Don't we see Odysseus fight for his life on every page? Rather, it emphasizes that an individual's lifespan is not infinite, so it is all the more important to make the most of the time you have.

Even the gods cannot prevent
the inevitable: death.

Then the two, the hero Telemachus and the glorious son of Nestor [Peisistratus], halted at the gateway of the palace, they and their two horses. And the lord Eteoneus came forth and saw them, the eager squire of glorious Menelaus; and he went through the hall to bear the tidings to the shepherd of the people. So, he came near and spoke to him winged words:

"Here are two strangers, Menelaus, fostered of Zeus, two men that are like the seed of great Zeus. But tell me, shall we unyoke for them their swift horses, or send them on their way to some other host, who will give them entertainment?"

Then, stirred to exceeding displeasure, fair-haired Menelaus spoke to him: "Before this it was not your custom to be a fool, Eteoneus, son of Boethous, but now like a child you talk folly. Surely we too many times ate the hospitable cheer of other men on our way here, hoping that Zeus would some day grant us respite from pain. No, unyoke the strangers' horses, and bring the men in, that they may feast."

So, he spoke, and the other hastened through the hall, and called to the other eager squires to follow along with him. They loosed the sweating horses from beneath the yoke and tied them at the stalls of the horses, and flung before them spelt, and mixed with it white barley. Then they tilted the chariot against the shining entrance walls, and led the men into the divine palace. But at the sight they marveled as they passed through the palace of the king, fostered by Zeus; for there was a gleam as of sun or moon over the high-roofed house of glorious Menelaus.

4.22–46

LESSON SIX

THE IMPORTANCE OF HOSPITALITY

"Surely we too many times ate the hospitable cheer
of other men on our way here, hoping that Zeus
would some day grant us respite from pain.
No, unyoke the strangers' horses, and bring
the men in, that they may feast."

4.31–34

One particularly important theme you will find woven throughout the *Odyssey* is *xenia*. *Xenia* is an Ancient Greek term that is most often translated as "hospitality" or "guest friendship." Essentially it is the concept of treating your guest like a friend, even if they are a stranger—particularly if they are a stranger. And when I say woven throughout, I mean it is the thread that binds the entire narrative together.

From Book One we have the importance of *xenia* pressed upon us by the poet. Athena travels down to Earth to visit the kingdom of Odysseus, only to be shunned by the suitors. When Telemachus spots their guest—she appears as a mortal man—he is disgusted by the other men's behavior and welcomes her into his home. This is the way in which, from Book One, Homer situates the characters of Telemachus and the suitors in opposition to one another. Telemachus as Odysseus' son shows respect for a core value of early Greek culture; meanwhile, the suitors treat their own host with nothing but animosity.

→

When Telemachus leaves home for the first time, he is welcomed by the kings of Pylos and Mycenae. Menelaus, in particular, is a strong proponent of *xenia*, welcoming both Telemachus and his companion Peisistratus into his home, despite having no knowledge of who they are. As we can see from the quotation on page 62, the prospect of turning them away is almost offensive to him, probably because *xenia* is itself a religious principle.

The act of hospitality is overseen by the god Zeus, also known as Zeus Xenios. In this role, he is believed to protect strangers and reward good hosts. Though it is a later myth told by the Roman poet Ovid, this is perfectly encapsulated in the story of Baucis and Philemon.

According to the myth, Zeus and Hermes go to Greece disguised as mortals seeking shelter. They are turned away by countless people until they come to the home of Baucis and Philemon. Despite being poor, the couple welcome the strangers into their home and share with them their food and wine. Because of their generosity, when Zeus comes to destroy the town, he allows Baucis and Philemon to survive.

Similarly, throughout Homer's epic, those who respect the laws of *xenia* are rewarded, while those who disregard them

To turn away a stranger, therefore, is more than just an act of unkindness in ancient Greece; it is one that dishonors the gods.

are punished. Telemachus who opens his home receives the same treatment from others. The suitors who take advantage of their hosts are slaughtered. Eumaeus who welcomes the disguised Odysseus to his farm is rewarded for his service. Polyphemus—who eats his guests—is blinded.

To turn away a stranger, therefore, is more than just an act of unkindness in ancient Greece; it is one that dishonors the gods. It is also worth considering what travel truly meant in both the Bronze Age and archaic Greece. To visit another city or country took not a matter of hours but days, weeks, months, or even years. The hospitality of others was often the only thing between a traveler and starvation. This is especially true in cases such as Odysseus' where a soldier is returning home from war.

Of course, context is key both when considering the role of *xenia* in antiquity, and how these lessons might be relevant to us. It would be irresponsible of me to suggest that you should invite strangers into your home, but that doesn't mean that we shouldn't treat unknown people with kindness, share with them what we have, and make them feel welcome. Perhaps, in the twenty-first century, *xenia* is about opening our minds as much as our homes.

LESSON SEVEN

WEALTH ISN'T WORTH IT

"Thus, you may understand, I have no joy in being lord of this wealth; and you may well have heard of this from your fathers, whosoever they may be, for greatly indeed did I suffer, and saw the ruin of a stately house, stored with much excellent treasure. Would that I dwelt in my halls with but a third part of this wealth, and that those men were safe who then perished in the broad land of Troy far from horse-pasturing Argos."

4.90–100

The second stop on Telemachus' personal quest is the kingdom of Menelaus in Mycenae. He has brought with him Peisistratus, the son of Nestor, and the two are treated to a lavish feast upon their arrival. As they eat, Peisistratus cannot help but comment on the wealth of Menelaus' home; even going so far as to compare it to the kingdom of Zeus himself. Upon hearing his guest's words, however, Menelaus is quick to jump in. For one, it would not do to offend the gods through comparison, but also because he wants these young men to understand that wealth comes at a price.

Generally speaking, wealth in the *Odyssey* is seen as a positive reflection of character. By Homeric logic, bravery leads to fame which leads to wealth. Yet Menelaus' words remind us of the inherent contradiction in this interpretation. For this Mycenaean king at least, renowned across the Mediterranean and beyond, wealth and fame do not make up for what he cannot have.

Did not the entire Trojan conflict begin because Helen, Menelaus' wife, was abducted by their guest? Menelaus then spent the better part of a decade waging war on the people of Troy, coming close to death on a number of occasions, and losing countless friends and family members along the way.

This fails to mention the aftermath of the Trojan War, when Menelaus sailed the seas for numerous years accumulating treasures. Meanwhile, his own brother Agamemnon returned

→

home from the war, only to be murdered by his wife and have his kingdom taken over by a usurper. Menelaus ponders, what if he had been there? Could he have saved him?

So, Menelaus tells Telemachus and Peisistratus that he would rather have a fraction of his current wealth if instead he could have the lives of those he has lost returned to them. Though his circumstances are specific, Menelaus' words certainly raise the question of what fame and money are truly worth. What are we willing to give up for them?

Here, we are not discussing the kind of "wealth" that can feed your family and heat your house. The riches that Menelaus has acquired surpass what any one person could ever need. Yes, they are impressive—they impress his guests and decorate his home—but they do not equate to happiness. They certainly weren't worth the loss of human life that facilitated them.

Menelaus' words offer us an important reminder, and a truth to hold onto. When we feel compelled to continuously seek out increasing wealth, what might we be sacrificing? Friends, family, health, or even the happiness of strangers? Because these are the things that matter, not empty riches.

Menelaus would
rather have a fraction
of his current wealth
if instead he could
have the lives of those
he has lost returned
to them.

NESTOR

When Telemachus sets out on his own quest toward the beginning of the *Odyssey*, the first man he visits is Nestor, king of Pylos. Why? The reasons are not just geographical: Nestor is the man who everyone turns to when they have questions, and questions are exactly what Telemachus has.

Nestor was the oldest of all the kings and generals who had gone to Troy alongside Odysseus two decades earlier. Due to his age, he could not fight on the ground but, never one to shy away from action, he led his men atop a horse-drawn carriage. Meanwhile, whenever the other Greeks found themselves in need of answers or advice, it was Nestor they turned to.

But how old is the king exactly? It is impossible to pinpoint Nestor's precise age, although notably there are tales in which he accompanied previous generations of heroes on their adventures, including Heracles and Jason. According to some later sources, including Hyginus' *Fabulae*, his lifespan was unnaturally long thanks to a blessing from Apollo. Basically, he has a lot of life experience.

When Telemachus visits Nestor, the elderly man is living a comfortable life alongside his wife Eurydice and their surviving children. Unlike many of his comrades who fought at Troy, Nestor's journey home had been relatively straightforward, and he has not suffered since his return. Following the fall of Troy, Nestor refused to engage in the ongoing quarrel between the brothers Agamemnon and Menelaus. He loaded his ship and took his men home. A plan that obviously worked out well.

→

"For to this end have you sailed over the sea, to seek tidings of your father—where the earth covered him, and what fate he met. But come now, go straight to Nestor, tamer of horses; let us learn what counsel he keeps hid in his breast. Beseech him yourself that he may tell you the very truth. A lie [he will not] utter, for he is wise indeed." 3.15–20

Telemachus, in his time
of need, has turned to
someone older and wiser
in search of advice.

Is it any wonder then that Telemachus goes straight to Nestor's door to ask after his father? Nestor informs the prince that to recount all that happened in Troy and the aftermath would take six years in total but, you know what, he'll give it a shot. He tells Telemachus of Odysseus' wisdom and how the two men often worked together throughout the war. He also shares with him what limited information he has regarding Odysseus' movements after the fighting—though this isn't much.

In many ways, this interaction between Telemachus and Nestor is an opportunity for Homer to recount the mythological events that precede the month in which his poem is set through its characters—a narrative technique of which the poet is particularly fond. That is not all it is, however. It is also a learning moment for Telemachus who, in his time of need, has turned to someone older and wiser in search of advice, advice that Nestor imparts through his recollections of the past. This is not unlike what we're doing here, though we might consider the *Odyssey* mythology rather than history.

During Telemachus' stay, Nestor encourages him to act. Like his father, he has Athena on his side, which is a gift he should not waste. Nestor's words are an attempt to instill in the young man some of the confidence he sorely lacks. Meanwhile, there is much that we as readers can also take away from this interaction.

It is probably something you've heard before—to respect your elders—and that is certainly a part of the dynamic at play in the interaction between Telemachus and Nestor, but I don't think this phrase really does it justice. What does "respect" really mean? All too often age seems to be accompanied by invisibility in the modern world. Yet, with the passing of time, it is important to remember that we do not lose our value—whichever side of the age divide we are on.

In Nestor we have a figure who has learned much from his time on Earth and, perhaps more importantly, is happy to share this knowledge. In Telemachus we have a relatively inexperienced young man who is able to recognize when someone else knows more than him. Nestor has also passed down some of his intelligence to his son Peisistratus. He even sends Peisistratus with Telemachus on the next leg of his journey, providing the prince with a reliable companion with whom he can exchange ideas, just as his father and Nestor once did at Troy.

LESSON EIGHT

DON'T GIVE UP

"Are you so very foolish, stranger, and slack of wit,
or are you of your own will remiss, and have pleasure
in suffering woes? So long are you pent in
the isle and can find no appointed end, and the
heart of your comrades grows faint."

4.371–4

Have you ever wondered to yourself why, when faced with so many obstacles—gods trying to sabotage them and monsters eating their friends—the heroes of Greek mythology are never tempted to just give up? I know the thought would have crossed my mind once or twice. Well, as it turns out, Menelaus at least isn't that different from you or I after all.

During the Spartan king's recollection of his own return trip from Troy, Menelaus describes how he found himself and his crew trapped on the island of Pharos. For twenty days they were stuck there due to the unforgiving winds that prevented them from sailing away, leaving them slowly running out of food and other supplies. So demoralized was Menelaus that he took to wandering aimlessly along the coast, while his comrades tried to catch fish. He is convinced that the gods are no longer listening to him and his prayers are pointless after so long. I imagine many of us can relate to this feeling of being helpless, hopeless, and despondent.

Except Menelaus was not as alone as he thought. For, as he walked alone along the beach, he was greeted by the goddess Eidothea, daughter of the sea god Proteus. She scorns Menelaus for giving up so easily, for wallowing in his misery when there

→

might yet be something he can do. She reminds him that it is not simply his own life at stake here, but that of his crew as well. Now is not the time to give up.

Simultaneously rallied by and resentful of the goddess' words, Menelaus asks her how they might escape the island then. More than happy to help, Eidothea explains that Menelaus must capture her father, Proteus, and force him to tell them how to cross the sea. And when Menelaus prompts her, she even tells him exactly how a mortal might capture a god.

Of course, at this point in the story we already know that Menelaus and his wife Helen make it back home safely. If they had not, there would be no one to tell Telemachus this tale. It will come as no surprise, therefore, that Eidothea's plan plays out just as she had suggested.

Menelaus' story is the perfect reminder that you never know what's around the corner. Even when things seem hopeless it is more often the case that we simply haven't considered every possibility. In order to turn things around we need to be willing to continue trying. In other words, we can't give up. And though we cannot all rely on the assistance of the ancient Greek gods, this doesn't mean that next time you're tempted to abandon all hope, you can't ask a friend to take on the role of Eidothea to help get you out of a slump; or perhaps you could simply imagine the sea goddess whispering encouraging insults in your ear.

Many of us are able to relate to this feeling of being helpless, hopeless, and despondent.

HELEN

Helen's story is one that everyone seems to know. Helen of Troy: the face that launched a thousand ships. Except this could hardly be a more reductive summary. Helen was, first of all, Helen of Sparta. She is the daughter of Zeus, king of the gods, and Leda, queen of Sparta. Leda's husband, King Tyndareus, meanwhile, raised Helen as his own.

From an early age, tales of Helen's beauty spread, and when it came time for her to wed she garnered a significant number of suitors. Kings from across Greece gathered to vie for her hand, including Menelaus and Odysseus. It is important to note, however, that these men were not purely interested in Helen's good looks. A marriage to Helen also meant a dowry from Tyndareus' kingdom: Helen's husband would automatically become king of Sparta.

All of this naturally caused some quarreling among Helen's suitors and Tyndareus worried whoever he chose would lead to fighting. It was Odysseus who came to him with a solution. He suggested that all the suitors swear a binding oath to defend whichever one of them won Helen's hand against violence. In exchange Odysseus was given the hand of Tyndareus' niece Penelope, and Menelaus was given Helen's.

We don't know much about Helen and Menelaus' early marriage, but they did have one child together: a daughter named Hermione. Their union becomes the subject of mythology once more when Helen is taken to Troy by Prince Paris. There are numerous attempts to explain how and why Helen went to Troy. Some posit that she was abducted; some that Aphrodite influenced her, so that she went willingly.

→

While he pondered thus in mind and heart, forth then from her fragrant high-roofed chamber came Helen, like Artemis of the golden distaff; and with her came Adraste, and placed for her a chair, beautifully wrought, and Alcippe brought a rug of soft wool and Phylo a silver basket, which Alcandre had given her, the wife of Polybus, who dwelt in Thebes of Egypt, where greatest store of wealth is laid up in men's houses. 4.120–27

There are even ancient authors who dedicated entire texts to exploring all the possible scenarios (see Gorgias' *Encomium of Helen*, ca. fifth century BCE). Within the Homeric epics, meanwhile, there are some figures who blame her, while others sympathize with her story. Even Helen herself is shown to struggle with complex feelings of anger, shame, resentment, and grief.

When we meet her in the *Odyssey*, however, she and Menelaus seem happy. The war is over, Paris is dead, and Helen has returned to her family. When Telemachus and Peisistratus arrive in Sparta, she is the first to recognize that Telemachus is Odysseus' son. This is despite the fact that her husband has sat and talked with the young prince for some time before she enters the room.

Over the course of Telemachus' visit, Helen comforts him with tales of his father's courage and cunning. She reminisces on her interactions with the hero during the war and how he ultimately devised her rescue. Then, when all three men are overcome by sorrow and unable to rest, she slips them a drug so that they might sleep easily.

Finally, as Telemachus readies himself to leave Sparta in Book Fourteen, the party spot an eagle in the sky. While Menelaus cannot grasp what this might mean, Helen immediately recognizes it as a promising omen from her father Zeus: an omen that predicts the success of Telemachus and Odysseus in Ithaca.

While the Helen of the twentieth and twenty-first centuries is all too often a one-dimensional damsel or adulteress, remembered primarily for her beautiful face, Homer's Helen is a complex and clever figure. This is also the Helen of wider Greek mythology. Occasionally time can smooth out stories and characters, wearing down their edges until they are something simple and easy to digest. And at times I worry that this is what has happened to Helen.

Helen is more than just her beauty. Homer knew that; it is time that has forgotten. Nor is she the only person, the only woman, historical or contemporary, ever to be reduced to her physical appearance. It is sadly all too common. Yet we do ourselves and others a disservice when we fall into this trap. And that is why, for me, the Helen of the *Odyssey* is a timely reminder to never judge a book by its cover or a person by their looks.

Helen is shown to struggle with complex feelings of anger, shame, resentment, and grief.

LESSON NINE

TREAT EVERYONE EQUALLY

"Surely you [did not listen] in olden days when you were children, when your fathers told what manner of man Odysseus was among them that begot you, in that he did no wrong in deed or word to any man in the land as the custom is of divine kings—one man they hate and another they love. Yet he never dealt intemperately at all with any man."

4.687–92

When Telemachus sets forth on his own quest, the suitors are horrified to hear of his departure. Together they form a plan to ambush the young prince on his return and end his life once and for all. Of course, they are overheard—they don't even try to hide their plotting—and a servant named Medon rushes to inform Penelope. It is upon greeting Medon that Penelope recites these words, pondering what the suitors might be up to this time.

Despite years of the suitors plaguing her, Penelope still struggles to understand how they could be so cruel. Did they not grow up in Ithaca? Did their own fathers not speak fondly of Odysseus? Did they not praise his fairness and his magnanimity?

In this moment Penelope specifically contrasts Odysseus with other rulers who are biased and selective, "one man they hate and another they love," treating the people around them differently depending on their mood. But not Odysseus.

→

Penelope doesn't have to remind us of the suitors' bad qualities. We have already seen that for ourselves. They are Odysseus' opposite in every way. He is fair where they are greedy; he is kind where they are cruel. This is important.

It is easy to be dazzled by a Hollywood actor dressed in Bronze Age armor and striding through a well-lit battlefield or captured by a speaker who harkens back to an era of bravery based on swords and shields. Yet this isn't why Odysseus is a role model. He's undoubtedly strong, but when it comes time for Penelope to praise her own husband, it is his fairness she chooses to emphasize. This is the quality that defines him.

In this way and many others, Homer's *Odyssey* is a book about kindness and respect. Not violence or conquest. After all, is the end goal not peace and harmony? Thus, if we are to begin to learn from the *Odyssey*, from the mythical figures who litter its pages, then surely this too is where we must begin. We must treat everyone with equal respect. We must give everyone an equal chance. And we must not treat one person better than another. This is what Odysseus would do.

Odysseus is fair where they are greedy; he is kind where they are cruel.

CALYPSO

While it famously takes Odysseus a decade to return home, he doesn't actually spend most of that time at sea. Seven whole years, in fact, are spent on the island of Ogygia as a captive of the nymph Calypso. Beyond the adventures of Odysseus, we do not know much about Calypso, yet in the *Odyssey* she has an incredibly important role to play. Starting with Odysseus' arrival on her shores.

Now, there is a reason Odysseus finds himself stranded in Ogygia for so long and it's not just the will of Calypso. In the second year of the hero's voyage home, he and his men moor their ship on the coast of Thrinacia, an island that belongs to the sun god Helios. This is where Helios keeps his renowned immortal cattle, which Odysseus warns his men not to harm, lest they anger the god. Oh, how things could have turned out so differently ...

When Poseidon forces the men to remain in Thrinacia for weeks on end, they grow desperate and sacrifice a selection of Helios' flock. This naturally angers Helios, who threatens to take the Sun into the Underworld and never shine its light on Earth again, should Zeus not avenge him. So, of course, the king of the gods is obliged to destroy Odysseus' ship with his lightning, killing everyone aboard except the man himself.

Odysseus survives and is washed ashore on Ogygia. He is rewarded with his life for warning his men against their actions, but as their leader Helios still demands that he be punished. This punishment comes in the form of a further delay to his journey home.

→

Now the fourth day came and all his work was done. And on the fifth the beautiful Calypso sent him on his way from the island after she had bathed him and dressed him in fragrant clothing. On the raft the goddess put a skin of dark wine, and another, a large one, of water, and provisions, too, in a bag. In it she put many good things to satisfy his heart, and sent him, too, a fair wind, gentle and warm. 5.262–68

In the end, Calypso cannot sway Odysseus.

This is not at all to diminish Calypso's role in Odysseus' imprisonment. At first, it does seem that the nymph and Odysseus enjoy each other's company. His words suggest that he once willingly joined her in her bed. Yet, by the time we meet our hero, it is evident that his feelings have changed. When exactly this change happened is unclear, but it is implied that it was quite some time ago. Calypso meanwhile struggles to accept that Odysseus does not love her the way she loves him.

The rest of the gods, meanwhile, have met to discuss Odysseus' fate, and thanks to Athena's advocacy Zeus has agreed that it is time for the hero to return home. Hermes, the messenger god, is sent to inform Calypso that she must finally free Odysseus, and who is she to argue with the king of the gods?

Of course, Calypso's obsession with Odysseus does not simply vanish just because Hermes tells her she must let him go. She informs Odysseus that she will no longer hold him against his will, but nevertheless attempts to bribe him into staying of his own accord. She even goes so far as to offer him immortality in exchange for his companionship.

In the end, Calypso cannot sway Odysseus. He has no interest in immortality. To him it is as good as death, for what makes life so sweet is that it will one day come to an end. Rather than remain isolated on Ogygia with nothing to do but while away the days, he desires to return to Ithaca and be reunited with his family. In other words, to live.

So, Odysseus sets to work building himself a raft and Calypso provides him with gifts he can actually use: food, drink, and other provisions, including a sail she has woven herself, a feat that would take one woman years in itself. In this way, Calypso gives Odysseus the means to return to Ithaca, even though she does so reluctantly.

Calypso's sorrow is a reminder to us all of the futility of holding on for too long. Instead, we must let go. We cannot force others to reciprocate our feelings and refusing to accept rejection will only hurt everyone involved. This lesson also applies to more than just unrequited love. Holding on to things for too long can be self-destructive. It can prevent us from moving forward and finding fulfilment. Letting things go, meanwhile, can free us and allow us to find true happiness.

LESSON TEN

SEE THINGS THROUGH

"My child, what a word has escaped the barrier of your teeth! Did you not yourself devise this plan, that in all truth Odysseus might take vengeance on these men at his coming? But concerning Telemachus, guide him in your wisdom, for you have the power, that all unscathed he may reach his native land, and the suitors may come back in their ship baffled in their purpose."

5.21–27

It seems that even gods and goddesses can feel a little forlorn in the Homeric world. For when we are reunited with Athena in Book Five of the *Odyssey*, she finds herself lamenting the fact that Odysseus remains on Calypso's Island, beaten down by his many trials, unable to carry on. She even shares her concerns with Zeus whose response, for all the beauty of Homer's poetry, is effectively, "What are you going to do about it then?" As he says to Athena, "Did you yourself not devise this plan?"

It is not that Zeus is unsympathetic to Athena or indeed Odysseus. Yet, he reminds his daughter that it was she who set herself the challenge of guiding the Greek hero home to be reunited with his family. He has helped, of course. The *Odyssey* rarely suggests anyone must go it alone entirely. But he also reminds Athena that if she is so invested in the hero's journey, she must be willing to see through what she herself began.

As mere mortals, meanwhile, I am sure we have all had moments like this. Where we have set ourselves a task or goal, yet stumbled when things got tough. Assuming I'm not alone, we've likely all started something that we gave up on halfway through. And maybe that was the right call. For none of this is to say that everything we try is going to be the right fit, or that we might not need to rethink and readjust depending on the circumstances. Yet, when it matters, when it's something we're passionate about or consider to be important, the words of Zeus can speak to more than just the deities of Olympus.

This is especially true when we have made a commitment to someone in the way Athena has. Without the goddess Odysseus' journey is doomed. Throughout the *Odyssey* it is she who convinces the gods to lend him a hand, offers him words of advice, and reminds him of his own strength and resilience when he needs it the most. It's a big responsibility, but one worth the pay-off if she is willing to see it through. Which, of course, she does.

Athena must be willing
to see through what
she herself began.

As for [Odysseus], for long the wave held him under, nor could he rise at once from beneath the onrush of the great wave, for the garments which beautiful Calypso had given him weighed him down. At length, however, he came up, and spat forth from his mouth the bitter brine which flowed in streams from his head. Yet even so he did not forget his raft, in distress though he was, but lunged after it amid the waves, and laid hold of it, and sat down in the middle of it, seeking to escape the doom of death; and the great seas bore the raft this way and that along their course. As when in autumn the North Wind bears the thistle tufts over the plain, and close they cling to one another, so did the winds bear the raft this way and that over the sea. Now the South Wind would fling it to the North Wind to be driven on, and now again the East Wind would yield it to the West Wind to drive.

But the daughter of Cadmus, Ino of the beautiful ankles, saw him, that is, Leucothea, who formerly was a mortal of human speech, but now in the depths of the sea has won a share of honor from the gods. She was touched with pity for Odysseus, as he wandered beset with troubles, and she rose up from the waters like a sea mew on the wing, and sat on the stoutly bound raft, and spoke, saying:

"Unhappy man, how is it that Poseidon, the Earth-shaker, has so astoundingly willed your pain, in that he sows for you the seeds of so many evils? Yet certainly he shall not utterly destroy you for all his rage. Instead, do as I say; you seem not to lack understanding. Strip off these garments, and leave your raft to be driven by the winds, while you by swimming with your hands strive to reach the land of the Phaeacians, where it is your fate to escape. Come, take this veil, and stretch it beneath your breast. It is immortal, and there is no fear that you shall suffer any hurt, or perish. But when with your hands you have laid hold of the land, untie it again and throw it into the wine-dark sea far from the land and yourself turn away."

5.319–51

LESSON ELEVEN

ACCEPT HELP

"Unhappy man, how is it that Poseidon, the earth-shaker, has so astoundingly willed your pain, in that he sows for you the seeds of so many evils? Yet certainly he shall not utterly destroy you for all his rage. Instead, do as I say."

5.339–42

Though the *Odyssey* gets its name from a single man, very little that happens throughout the epic is achieved by Odysseus alone. Odysseus, Telemachus, Penelope, you name it, all the characters of the *Odyssey* consistently rely on the help of others to achieve their goals. This is such a regular feature of Homer's poem that there were almost too many examples to pick from when choosing which quote to use for this lesson. In the end, though, I thought it was the words of Leucothea that best encapsulated this aspect of the *Odyssey*.

Odysseus meets Leucothea in Book Five when he finds himself adrift at sea. The winds whip his raft back and forth, while Poseidon's waters prevent him from reaching dry land. All seems lost, that is, until another deity offers him assistance.

Leucothea was once a mortal queen named Ino, but was transformed into a sea goddess by Zeus, long before the events of the *Odyssey*. When she comes across Odysseus she is moved by his plight. She recognizes that he is no ordinary sailor lost at sea, but someone who has angered Poseidon enough to bring down his wrath. Despite this, Leucothea offers to help him.

→

"Do as I say," Leucothea tells Odysseus, offering him her veil so that it might protect him. Of course, Odysseus could say no. As much as Leucothea's words read like a command, there is no divine compulsion behind them. It is up to Odysseus whether he accepts her help or not, which, of course, he does.

Were it not for this early example of accepting the help of another the *Odyssey* might have been much shorter; Odysseus would undoubtedly have died at sea should he have rejected Leucothea's assistance.

Nor is this the last time Odysseus will receive help throughout the *Odyssey*. Never is this painted as a bad thing, though. Odysseus is wise to accept help; not everyone is so lucky.

So, the next time you're convinced the only way to accomplish anything is to do it alone, remember not just Odysseus but the whole cast of the *Odyssey*. Accepting the help of others doesn't minimize your achievements. Rather, it speaks to your understanding of what a situation requires, and how more heads are often better than one.

All the characters of the *Odyssey* consistently rely on the help of others to achieve their goals.

LESSON TWELVE

CRY LIKE A HERO

But [Hermes did not find] the great-hearted Odysseus within; for he sat weeping on the shore, in his accustomed place, racking his heart with tears and groans and griefs. There he would look out over the unresting sea, shedding tears.

5.82–84

When we first meet the hero Odysseus in Homer's *Odyssey,* he is not battling Trojans, slaying monsters, or concocting cunning plans; he is sitting on the shores of Ogygia staring out to sea. It has been seventeen years since he last saw his home, his wife, or his son. He is shipwrecked and alone, stranded on an unknown island. In this moment he is without hope. And so, he weeps.

While Odysseus' precise circumstances might be unfamiliar to us—personally I have never had to maneuver a ship through a narrow strait bordered by two mythical beasts—his emotions are likely not. At some point or another, many of us will feel lost, lonely, or otherwise overwhelmed by emotion.

Though it might be tempting to bottle up these feelings, to try to pretend we are unaffected by the world, this is not the approach taken in the Homeric epics. We often encounter figures in the *Odyssey* weeping inconsolably. Something that is perhaps even more true of the *Iliad* where war and tears are inevitable companions.

→

Nor is it just in moments of sadness we see these tears fall. When Odysseus is eventually reunited with his son Telemachus, both father and child partake in a tearful embrace: "Telemachus, flinging his arms about his good father, wept and shed tears, and in the hearts of both arose a longing for lamentation." (16.212)

Beyond Odysseus' example, the consensus from modern psychologists and therapists seems pretty irrefutable: crying is good for you. To acknowledge our emotions is an important step in learning to work with them. It is this that prevents powerful and sometimes difficult feelings from subsuming us, not pushing them down to some deep recesses we cannot reach. And yes, sometimes this looks like sitting on the beach and having a good old-fashioned Homeric sob.

In the world of Homer's epics, to hold back tears is not a sign of strength. We all experience grief and sadness. We all struggle at times. We should, therefore, all be able to cry. In fact, if Odysseus' story is anything to go by, to cry is not just human, it is heroic.

Many of us will feel lost,
lonely, or otherwise
overwhelmed by emotion.

POSEIDON

Though I would hesitate to describe any god as a villain in ancient Greek mythology—for all the horrific things they do they still receive the respect of their worshippers—I think it's fair to say that Poseidon is definitely an antagonist in Odysseus' story. And what an enemy to have ...

Poseidon is undoubtedly one of the most powerful gods on Olympus. The son of the Titans Kronos and Rhea and the brother of Zeus, he could even have been king of the heavens himself, if he'd been luckier when drawing straws for rule over Earth's three dominions. Zeus' longest straw gave him the heavens, the shortest for Hades gave him the Underworld, and with Poseidon in the middle, he was granted the seas.

The thing is, if your civilization is dependent on the sea for much of its travel and trade, this makes Poseidon pretty important. Hence, he was regularly prayed to by fishermen, sailors, and those who lived by the coast. Whether it be for safe sailing conditions or a bountiful catch, Poseidon was the one to ask and should you anger him he could put your life in danger in a multitude of ways. Unfortunately, this was exactly what Odysseus did.

During his journey home from Troy, Odysseus encountered the Cyclops known as Polyphemus. The meeting was a not a happy one, however, as Polyphemus first ate a handful of Odysseus' friends before Odysseus blinded the Cyclops in order to escape his clutches. So, mistakes on both sides really.

→

And at once [Athena] prayed earnestly to the lord Poseidon: "Hear me, Poseidon, Earth-bearer, and do not begrudge in answer to our prayer to fulfill these requests. To Nestor, first of all, and to his sons vouchsafe renown, and then to the rest grant gracious requital for this glorious hecatomb, to all the men of Pylos. Grant furthermore that Telemachus and I return home having accomplished that for which we came here with our swift black ship." 3.53-61

We would do well not to view our own challenges in black and white terms either.

What Odysseus did not consider was that Polyphemus was the son of Poseidon. Thus, from that point on Poseidon was ill-inclined to the hero and did everything in his power to sabotage Odysseus' journey.

In this way, Poseidon is the overarching obstacle of Odysseus' quest. As readers, we rarely see the god appear in person, yet he is ever-present throughout the narrative. In the form of stormy skies and treacherous waves, he shipwrecks Odysseus, kills his crew, and prevents him from reaching home countless times.

Despite all this, Poseidon cannot be called a villain. As we see in the quote on page 106, even wise Athena acknowledges his position and prays to him for Telemachus' safety. We would do well not to view our own challenges in black and white terms either. As readers we can appreciate where Poseidon's anger comes from—Odysseus did blind his son—even if his subsequent response seems extreme. Poseidon reminds us that things are never as simple as they might appear. Even if we disagree with someone's decisions, trying to understand what might have led them to their conclusions, rather than viewing them as a caricatured monster, can help us better communicate and work through our differences.

Poseidon can also help us approach untamable powers outside of our control. Like the ocean, there will be forces in life that can be both a blessing and a curse. They can also be completely arbitrary, unchangeable, and unfair.

While we can understand Poseidon's motivation for revenge in Odysseus' case, his other whims may seem more vindictive. He punishes the Phaeacians after they respect the laws of guest friendship and help Odysseus. Yet, because of Poseidon's feelings toward the Greek king, they are punished harshly; the god turns an entire ship of men to stone, so that they sink to the bottom of the sea.

For all that this seems unjust, this incident is a reminder of the capricious and seemingly unfair way that life can play out. Sometimes we have to accept that things are simply outside of our control. We cannot change the weather or force the sea to do our bidding, and nor should we try to. We can only strive to do our best; to pick ourselves up and carry on despite the challenges we face along the way.

LESSON THIRTEEN

IT'S THE SMALL THINGS

Then when they had had their joy of food, she and her handmaids, they threw off their headgear and fell to playing at ball, and white-armed Nausicaa was leader in the song. And even as Artemis, the archer, roves over the mountains, along the ridges of lofty Taygetus or Erymanthus, joying in the pursuit of boars and swift deer, and the wood nymphs, daughters of Zeus who bears the aegis, share her sport, and Leto is glad at heart.

6.99–107

For all that the *Odyssey* is full of journeys to the Underworld, encounters with mythical beasts, and conversations with powerful deities, it is also a tale tied together by ordinary moments. We read about characters recovering in warm baths, men relaxing with a game of checkers, friends conversing over shared meals, and young women playing ball games while singing.

When we first meet the princess Nausicaa in Book Six, she has taken it upon herself to take her brothers' clothing to be washed in the stream. While there, she and her maids eat a lunch provided by the queen, pass a ball between them, and sing songs in the afternoon sun. This moment and others like it are not simply filler to bulk out Homer's word count. They are as important, if not more so, than the grand adventures had by the epic's hero. For this is what Odysseus yearns for: normalcy; the little things; the simple pleasures.

As we know, Odysseus' journey is defined by his desire to return home and be reunited with his family. He does not long for war or battle. He didn't even want to travel to Troy in the first place. Nausicaa's contentment as she watches over her maids and frolics alongside them is symbolic of this greater theme that presents itself throughout the poem. It is these moments of small joy, friendship, or connection that make life worth living. They can also help us better relate to the characters of Homer's epic, whose battles with Cyclopes and dealings with gods may seem so far from our own reality. And just as these moments resonate with us, so they likely also did with ancient audiences. Thus, we are connected through time, and reminded that we can continue to learn from this text millennia on.

It is easy when we are consuming media, whether literature or film, to get lost in the fantastical elements, the action-packed adventures, and fool ourselves into thinking this is the point. Of course, adventures are exciting but aren't they all the more so for these little moments along the way? Admiring the beautiful architecture, trying the local cuisine, or striking up a conversation with someone you've never met before.

Time and time again, the *Odyssey* reminds its audience that whether you're far from home, or in the comfort of your own backyard, it is important to revel in the simple pleasures. For these are what matter most.

This is a tale tied
together by
ordinary moments.

NAUSICAA

Nausicaa, daughter of King Alcinous and Queen Arete, princess of Phaeacia. Often grouped together with Calypso and Circe as one of Odysseus' potential love interests during his journey, she also typically comes away from these discussions looking ten times better than her literary sisters. But why exactly is that? And who is Nausicaa beyond her interaction with Odysseus?

Aside from the *Odyssey* we don't know much about Nausicaa, particularly when it comes to her life before and after meeting Odysseus. The ancient scholia tell us that the Classical Greek playwright Sophocles penned a tragedy entitled *Nausicaa,* but sadly the narrative is lost to time. Yet, despite limited records, she has continued to be a subject of fascination in Classical culture, from nineteenth-century paintings to twentieth-century novels.

We first meet Nausicaa in Book Six of Homer's epic when she is awoken from a rather inspiring dream. In said dream the goddess Athena comes to her and tells her that her wedding day is fast approaching. Notably, the princess is not engaged, but Athena preys on the fact that Nausicaa has recently reached an age when marriage is what is expected of her. The goddess continues, saying that in order to properly prepare for her impending nuptials, Nausicaa must take her clothes and those of her future wedding party to the river to be washed. You wouldn't want to wear dirty clothes to your wedding, would you?

→

Even so Odysseus was about to enter the company of the fair-tressed maidens, naked though he was, for need had come upon him. And terrible he seemed to them, all befouled with brine, and they fled in fear, one here, one there, along the jutting sand spits. Alone the daughter of Alcinous kept her place, for in her heart Athene put courage, and took fear from her limbs. She stood and faced him. 6.135–41

So, it is with marriage in her mind that Nausicaa travels to the river outside the city walls with her handmaidens to wash her family's clothing. Of course, Athena has no real interest in Nausicaa's future wedding. She is motivated only by her desire to assist Odysseus, who just so happens to have recently washed up on the shores of Phaeacia.

As the women are readying themselves to return home, Odysseus appears from the bushes, a stranger, naked, and covered in seawater. Is it any wonder that they respond with fear? All but Nausicaa, that is. This is one of the moments that has ensured Nausicaa's memory lives on. For rather than run, she stands tall before this strange man and listens to his plea.

Impressed by his character, Nausicaa is quick to offer Odysseus assistance. She gives him food and clothes and allows him to wash himself off in the river. Further she explains how to best impress her parents, so they might welcome him into the palace as their guest. Her first instinct is kindness and, though she is partially reliant on her parents, to offer Odysseus her hospitality, qualities we have already seen Homer admires.

Let us not forget, though, that Nausicaa came to the river with a wedding on her mind. It will likely come as no surprise, therefore, that she turns to her companions and whispers that she would be lucky to marry a man such as this. A thought her father shares, for he eventually goes on to offer Odysseus his daughter's hand in marriage.

Odysseus, of course, is more interested in returning to Ithaca and his existing wife. After this first interaction we also never see Odysseus and Nausicaa alone again. In contrast with Calypso, who refuses to let Odysseus go, and Circe, whose first instinct is to harm the hero, Nausicaa and her family welcome Odysseus with open arms and no expectations. Marriage is certainly on the table, but it is never pushed upon their visitor. Their hospitality is unconditional, as is Nausicaa's kindness.

There is much we might admire in Nausicaa during our brief meeting with her. Her bravery, her kindness, and her openness. One point I have yet to touch on, however, is her wise approach to laundry. Yes, that's right. I couldn't end this profile without mentioning that at least two ancient writers who mention Nausicaa besides Homer do so because of where she washes her clothes. Both the Greek Plutarch (*Moralia*.627) and Roman Macrobius (*Saturnalia*.7.25), comment that the princess was wise to choose the river and not the ocean, for the latter would only leave her clothes greasy and covered in salt. Truly, Nausicaa is the perfect example of how we can all learn something different from figures in mythology.

Rather than run,
Nausicaa stands
tall before this
strange man
and listens to
his plea.

LESSON FOURTEEN

DON'T TAKE YOUR PARTNER FOR GRANTED

"For nothing is greater or better than this, than when a man and a woman keep house together sharing one heart and mind, a great grief to their foes and a joy to their friends; while their own fame is unsurpassed."

6.183–85

The *Odyssey* is many things—from heroic adventure to spiritual journey—but is it not also a romance? For every time Homer writes of Odysseus' quest to return to Ithaca, the poet also reminds us that what the hero desires most is to be reunited with his wife, Penelope.

Throughout the *Odyssey*, neither Odysseus nor Penelope ever forgets their spouse; often regaling the reader and other characters of the qualities they admire in the other. From their minds to their faces, there is nothing the two don't value in each other.

In this scene, Odysseus addresses the princess Nausicaa, who has helped him in his time of need. Washed ashore, alone and starving, on the island of Phaeacia, Odysseus receives new clothes from the princess and advice on how to win over her parents, the king and queen. As a thank you, Odysseus wishes her success in finding the kind of love he himself has with Penelope. For, as he says, "nothing is greater than ... a man and a woman ... sharing one heart and mind."

→

Neither Odysseus nor Penelope ever forgets their spouse.

Obviously, you don't need to be in a heterosexual relationship for Homer's or Odysseus' words to ring true. Making sure we show our appreciation for the ones we love is integral to any healthy relationship. Even after decades together, neither Odysseus nor Penelope takes the other for granted, yet for many this isn't the case. Over time we can forget how important it is to remind our partners what they mean to us. To extol their virtues and do things for them that show our appreciation.

One even wonders if a few other ill-fated relationships in Greek mythology might have worked out better if they had taken a leaf out of Odysseus and Penelope's book. Well, it might be too late for them, but it certainly doesn't have to be for us. Channel mythology's strongest couple and go tell your partner you love them. Pay them a compliment. Cook them a meal. Do something without asking. It doesn't have to be big, but making sure that you show someone you appreciate them in small ways every day is the surest way to maintain a love fit for epic poetry. You're a team after all.

POLYPHEMUS

Of all of Odysseus' foes, Polyphemus may be the most famous. Between his appearance, actions, and the way in which Odysseus escapes him, he really does stand out. No, this is not a giant joke. Well, maybe it is a giant joke. For Polyphemus is, of course, a Cyclops.

The Cyclopes are a race of giants in ancient Greek mythology, distinctive because they have a single large eye in the center of their face. Aside from their appearance, however, not all Cyclopes share a single origin. In the work of Hesiod, another famous Greek poet from the eighth or seventh century BCE, the Cyclopes were the sons of Ouranos (Sky) and Gaia (Earth)—the grandparents of Zeus. They were also responsible for crafting Zeus' legendary thunderbolts. Polyphemus, meanwhile, is the son of Poseidon and a nymph named Thoosa. Rather than forging weaponry, he lives the life of a shepherd.

In Homer's *Odyssey*, Polyphemus lives in the caves of an unidentified island—though the playwright Euripides places them in Sicily—alongside his fellow Cyclopes. The names and lineage of these other Cyclopes is never mentioned. Here Polyphemus tends to his flock of sheep and presumably lives a relatively simple life, something that seemed to fascinate later writers like Theocritus from the third century BCE, who took to writing pastoral poetry about Polyphemus and his love life.

Polyphemus' love life is certainly not of interest to Odysseus. When he and his crew arrive on the Cyclopes' island, they stow away in a cave and feast on its contents. This is not

→

"From [Polyphemus'] pitiless heart he made no answer, but sprang up and laid his hands upon my comrades. Two of them together he seized and dashed to the earth like puppies, and their brains flowed forth upon the ground and wetted the earth. Then he cut them limb from limb and made ready his supper, and ate them like a mountain-nurtured lion, leaving nothing—ate the entrails, and the flesh, and the bones and marrow." 9.287–98

one of Odysseus' best decisions. His companions tried to insist they gather any necessities and head off immediately, but Odysseus believes they can rely on the Cyclopes' hospitality and decides they should stay.

When Polyphemus returns to his cave with his flock, he takes a while to notice his guests but notice them he does. Rather than welcome them to his table and share his home with them, however, he picks up a handful of Odysseus' men and eats them whole. As I mentioned previously, eating the provisions in the cave was not the best decision.

We hear this story from Odysseus second hand as he narrates it to the Phaeacians many years later. During his recollection he reflects on the ways in which Polyphemus and the Cyclopes contrast with others he met on his journey, including his hosts. Polyphemus' behavior flies in the face of one of the *Odyssey*'s central values: *xenia* or hospitality. Odysseus characterizes the actions of Polyphemus as violent, uncivilized, and an affront to Zeus, god of *xenia*.

To further hammer home this point, Odysseus then recounts how he and his men escaped the Cyclops. Relying on his quick thinking, Odysseus offers Polyphemus wine from the skin they carry with them. Polyphemus' mistake is not simply that he accepts the wine, but the fact that he drinks it undiluted, because ancient Greek wine was incredibly strong and most people drank it watered down.

Drunk on wine, Polyphemus passes out, allowing Odysseus and his men the opportunity to blind him using a hot stake. Therefore, the next morning, when Polyphemus lets his flock out to roam, he is unable to see the men hanging beneath the bellies of his sheep, thereby allowing them to escape.

In summary, Polyphemus eats human flesh, drinks too much, and is an all-round bad host. The Cyclopes also receive criticism from Odysseus for living in caves, having no laws, and creating nothing for themselves.

Now, I think it is important to acknowledge here that judging societies and civilizations who organize themselves differently from your own is not admirable. This is not the lesson I want you to take away from this tale. Rather, Polyphemus' actions serve as a contrast to the ideal host that Homer depicts elsewhere in the *Odyssey*, and which the ancient Greeks prized so highly. Polyphemus provides an example of what *not* to do, not because he is a shepherd or doesn't own a ship, but because he abuses his power, uses his strength to harm others, and, well, eats people.

Polyphemus' behavior flies in the face of one of the *Odyssey*'s central values: *xenia* or hospitality.

LESSON FIFTEEN

REMEMBER THE PAST

But when they had put from them the desire for food and drink, the Muse moved the [bard] to sing of the glorious deeds of men, from that lay of which the fame had then reached broad heaven.

8.72–75

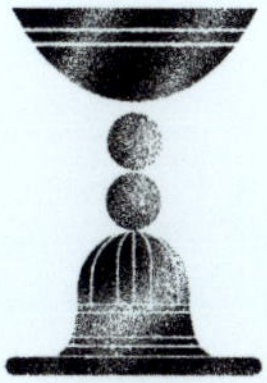

The *Odyssey* is not a chronological narrative. It is a story told through flashbacks and recollections. As you know, Homer's epic only really begins at the end; during the hero's final year at sea before he eventually returns home. Meanwhile, it has been almost two decades since Odysseus has seen his family, and a lot has happened in that time. An abduction, a war, a conquest, and countless family reunions. Throughout the *Odyssey*, we learn of these incidents through the sharing of stories that recollect the past.

Remembrance is a constant theme throughout the *Odyssey*. Sometimes this looks like Odysseus recounting his many woes at sea, while on other occasions performers entertain audiences with songs of the Trojan War.

In the quote accompanying this lesson we join Odysseus at the Phaeacian court, where all have just enjoyed a good meal, and are settling down to listen to a bard sing of times gone by. It's a recognizable scene—perhaps you have also enjoyed eating and drinking with friends or family, before starting to reminisce and share memories. In other parts of the story, Telemachus

→

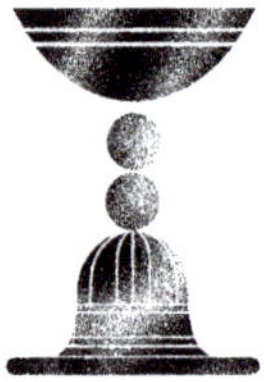

gets to know his absent father through the memories of others, while for Penelope memory keeps her husband alive. Shared recollections can often help us better understand something we haven't experienced, or allow us to feel closer to someone we know.

And in its own way this is also the purpose of the *Odyssey* itself: to remember a mythological time gone by. Though the truth of Homer's poetry is to be doubted, riddled with inconsistencies and impossible details as it is, that does not detract from the fact that in antiquity these events were presented as history.

The *Odyssey* tells us, there is value in each of these acts of remembrance. Through remembering the past we can connect with others, alive or dead. We can find comfort in the memories of loved ones who are no longer with us. We might be reminded of the things we have overcome and better appreciate where we find ourselves now. In remembering the past, Homer tells us, we honor those who came before as well as ourselves and all we have done. Perhaps even more importantly, we can learn from it, just as we learn from the *Odyssey* itself.

We learn of these
incidents through the
sharing of stories
that recollect the past.

CIRCE

Goddess? Nymph? Witch? Or all of the above? Circe is a fascinating figure both in the *Odyssey* and wider Greek mythology. She is also incredibly hard to pin down.

Born to the Titan sun god Helios and the ocean nymph Perse, her siblings include Aeëtes (king of Colchis and father of Medea) and Pasiphaë (queen of Crete and mother of the Minotaur). Unlike her royal siblings, Circe lives on a relatively deserted island called Aeaea alongside a group of nymphs who act as her companions. Here she is said to practice *pharmakeia*, or magic.

Though technically a goddess by birth, we have limited evidence for the worship of Circe in antiquity. Her veneration generally appears to have been small scale and localized, as with other minor figures in Greek religion. In the story of Odysseus, however, her role is pivotal.

In the early days of Odysseus' return trip from Troy, he and his crew dock their ship in the harbor of Aeaea. For two days they remain there, eating and drinking, until on the third day Odysseus decides to seek out civilization. After wandering for a while he climbs a nearby hill to survey the land and spots a single dwelling. Cautious of showing up at a stranger's home alone, however, he returns to his ship and sends a group of his men to investigate further. A tough break for them, let me tell you.

→

"I went my way to the house of Circe, and many things did my heart darkly ponder as I went. So I stood at the gates of the fair-tressed goddess. There I stood and called, and the goddess heard my voice. She came out at once and opened the bright doors and called me in; and I went with her, my heart deeply troubled. She brought me in and made me sit ... And she prepared me a potion in a golden cup, that I might drink, and put in it a drug, with evil purpose in her heart." 10.307–17

When the men arrive at their destination, they are greeted by Circe. However, Circe's hospitality doesn't exactly meet the Homeric ideal. They are invited into her home and served food that has been drugged. As soon as the men have finished their meal Circe strikes them with her wand and turns them into pigs. Specifically, they take on the body of pigs but retain their human minds. In this way they are aware of what has befallen them as Circe locks them in her pen, a passage I always find particularly visceral.

Of course, Odysseus begins to grow suspicious when his men don't return and sets out to find them. This is when he is visited by another god: Hermes. Hermes informs Odysseus what has befallen his crew and warns him he will suffer the same fate if he doesn't follow the god's instructions. First, he gives Odysseus a herb that will negate the power of Circe's potion, should he consume it. Then the god tells him to draw his sword and rush her the moment she raises her wand. This is when Circe will invite him into her bed, but before he does so he must make the goddess swear an oath never to harm him.

Odysseus follows Hermes' instructions to the letter, and from that moment on the fearsome goddess becomes a powerful ally, rather than a foe. Circe frees the men from their torment, bathes them, clothes them, and lets them feast. For an entire year Odysseus and his men enjoy lives of plenty, thanks to Circe's hospitality.

It's so pleasant, in fact, that Odysseus almost forgets where he is headed. After his crew remind him that he must return to Ithaca, however, he goes to Circe and asks for her assistance once more. Like any good host, Circe realizes when it is time for her guests to leave, and so she eagerly agrees.

Circe is the perfect reminder that people can surprise you. This is why second chances are so important.

Circe informs Odysseus that in order for his journey to be successful, he must first travel to the Underworld and speak with the seer Tiresias, and provides detailed instructions on how to find him. She also warns him of the dangers they will encounter along the way. While Odysseus is certainly cunning, let us not forget that it is Circe who explains to him how best to avoid the Sirens as well as the monsters Scylla and Charybdis, credit modern adaptations all too often fail to give her.

Given the significant role she plays in the *Odyssey*, there is a lot we can take away from Circe. Not only does she feed and host Odysseus and his men, but she is also full of sage advice. Yet, what is probably most striking about Circe's appearance in Homer's epic, is that her initial introduction positions her as an antagonist rather than a friend.

When Circe turns Odysseus' crew into pigs, you would be forgiven for regarding her as a villain. In the end, however, she is integral to Odysseus' safe return to Ithaca. Circe is the perfect reminder that people can surprise you. This is why second chances are so important. Would Odysseus have come up with the idea of putting wax in his crews' ears when sailing past the Sirens without her? I suppose we'll never know, but what is more important is that he didn't have to.

LESSON SIXTEEN

VALUE THE ARTS

"Herald, take and give this portion to Demodocus,
that he may eat, and I will greet him, despite
my grief. For among all men that are upon the
Earth [bards] win honor and reverence, for
the Muse has taught them the paths of song,
and loves the tribe of minstrels."

8.477–81

Throughout the *Odyssey*, Homer dedicates a not insignificant number of lines to the praise of artists. This may well not come as a surprise given that Homer was a poet himself. Nevertheless, given that I am discussing said poem in a book, one that you are reading, it seems only right to highlight this aspect of the *Odyssey*.

During his stay in Phaeacia, Odysseus is treated to the poetry of a bard named Demodocus, who recounts the events of the Trojan War. His words tap into Odysseus' pain and bring him to tears. For this Odysseus insists that Demodocus' meal be prioritized, for the bard deserves to be honored above all others.

Nor is this the only point in the narrative where Homer highlights the importance of artists and performers. Later, in Book Seventeen, for example, the swineherd Eumaeus compares bards to healers and seers. These men—though of course they can also be women—he claims are among the few everyone on Earth desires to be visited by.

This respect for poets is one which reflects wider ancient Greek values. After all, are the arts not aspects of the gods themselves? From the muses whom we have already discussed to Apollo, the god of music, inspiration came from the heavens.

→

And it didn't simply go one way. Ordinary Greeks regularly used art as a form of worship. They carved statues of their gods and staged theatrical competitions as part of religious festivals, to give just two examples. This was a result of the inherent value placed on art and literature by the Greeks.

Meanwhile, in our modern world, I have found it not uncommon to hear the arts derided as frivolous or unimportant. This, however, could not be further from the truth. It is through the arts that we learn about the past; about ourselves; about others. We imagine possible futures. We explore complex ideas. We sharpen our minds. Through art we are able to grow as individuals and communities.

Look at us now, still reading and discussing this one poem thousands of years since its composition. Art matters.

If you picked up this book, I'd like to think you're already some way—maybe all the way—to championing this idea. That you appreciate the value of art in all its forms. Even then, however, I know how easy it can be to dismiss our own artistic expression. We put it on the back burner. Deprioritize our creativity. Diminish our own capacity. All of this despite the ways in which it can improve our lives. Well, let this be your reminder to celebrate your creativity, because Homer certainly would.

The bard deserves
to be honored
above all others.

TIRESIAS

When Odysseus travels to the Underworld in Book Eleven it is for one very specific purpose: to speak with the blind seer Tiresias. Evidently, Tiresias at this point in Greek mythology is dead (or he wouldn't be in the Underworld), but prior to this, his life had been quite eventful.

It all began when a young Tiresias was walking through the mountains and came across two snakes engaged in intercourse. For whatever reason, disgust perhaps, he struck them with his stick, and so invited the wrath of Hera. As punishment, the goddess turned Tiresias into a woman. For many years Tiresias lived as a woman, even marrying and having children.

Then the day came when Tiresias encountered two snakes copulating once again. Sources vary, but she either repeated her previous actions, or this time left the animals alone—in both versions the result was Hera transforming her into a man once more.

This experience made Tiresias uniquely placed in the eyes of the gods. For when Zeus and Hera found themselves arguing over who gained more pleasure from sex—men or women—Tiresias seemed the obvious person to ask. The issue for Tiresias was that no matter what answer he gave, someone was going to be upset. So, when he informed the pair that Zeus was correct—women gain more pleasure—Hera was angry enough to blind him where he stood.

Zeus, meanwhile, felt bad for Tiresias and gave him the gift of prophecy. Thus, we reach his role in the *Odyssey*. Even in death, Circe describes Tiresias as steadfast and reasoned. Unlike the other souls in the Underworld, he retains his

→

"Son of Laertes, sprung from Zeus, [wily Odysseus], remain now no longer in my house against your will; but you must first complete another journey, and come to the house of Hades and dread Persephone, to seek prophecy from the ghost of Theban Tiresias, the blind seer, whose mind remains steadfast. To him even in death Persephone has granted reason, that he alone should have understanding, but the others flit about as shadows." 10.488–95

Tiresias continues to share
what he knows with others,
even in death.

cognizance. When the dead gather around Odysseus most have lost their minds and can only communicate once they have drunk the blood of the sacrificed animals. Not so for Tiresias.

Tiresias is another figure in the *Odyssey* whose appearance is somewhat brief, but important. Tiresias explains to Odysseus that he incited the ire of Poseidon when he blinded his son Polyphemus. This is why his journey has been so tumultuous. Still, if he follows the seer's advice, the hero will return to Ithaca. The same goes for his crew: should they themselves hope to reach home, then they must not harm the cattle of the sun god Helios when they encounter them.

Finally, Tiresias informs our hero that even when he returns to Ithaca and slays his wife's suitors, his trials will not be over. This is when Odysseus must set out on another journey, carrying an oar until he meets a man who calls it a "winnowing fan" because he knows nothing of seafaring. This is where Odysseus should sacrifice a ram, a bull, and a boar to the god Poseidon to finally appease his wrath. Unfortunately, the *Odyssey* ends with Odysseus in Ithaca, so we do not see this final journey unfold for ourselves.

Predictions of the future are not all that Tiresias tells Odysseus. When the hero asks how he might communicate with his dead mother, the seer tells him he must allow her to drink the blood of the sacrificial animals he has brought.

Their interaction might be short, but through Odysseus and Tiresias' conversation we learn that the seer is knowledgeable on various topics. Nor does he hold this knowledge close to his chest. Rather, Tiresias continues to share what he knows with others, even in death and in spite of his less than positive experiences with the gods in the past.

As readers we also witness what happens when Tiresias' good advice is ignored. For, despite Odysseus' protestations, his men do indeed slaughter Helios' cattle, ultimately leading to their own demise. Tiresias is, therefore, the perfect example of why knowledge matters. If we ignore the information offered to us by others, whether through arrogance or recklessness, we risk suffering the consequences.

Equally, when you do have information regarding an issue someone else might not, it is important to share it with others. Even if it seems insignificant to you, it might be exactly what someone else needs to hear. Never underestimate the value of sharing what you know.

LESSON SEVENTEEN

CELEBRATE YOUR TALENTS

"For we are not flawless boxers or wrestlers, but in the foot race we run swiftly, and we are the best seamen; and always to us is the banquet dear, and the lyre, and the dance, and changes of clothes, and warm baths, and the couch. But come now, all you who are the best dancers of the Phaeacians, make sport, that the stranger may tell his friends on reaching home how far we surpass others in seamanship and in fleetness of foot, and in the dance and in song."

8.244–54

During Odysseus' stay with the Phaeacians their king, Alcinous, decides to host a series of games to demonstrate his people's prowess to their guest. At first, Alcinous and his men are convinced they excel in every sport, until Odysseus takes his turn and proves his worth. For no man can throw the discus as far as our hero. Yet Odysseus concedes that he stands no chance in outstripping his hosts in a race. Thus, Alcinous makes his speech regarding where his people excel and, importantly, do not.

By the end of this exchange, everyone seems to agree on at least one thing: no one needs to be good at everything. Alcinous takes pride in his people's many talents. They are incomparable sailors and run with lightning speed. They appreciate good food and dance beautifully. All of these things and more deserve to be celebrated as they have dedicated much time and energy to perfecting their skills. He also accepts, however, that they are not number one in everything.

→

On an individual note, Odysseus' words parallel those of Alcinous. The Phaeacians are superior runners, while his strength cannot compare to heroes such as Heracles. He is happy to celebrate what he is good at but does not deny that others have bested him elsewhere.

Both men are good examples of how we need not be the best at everything. We don't even have to be good at everything. Rather than dwelling on what we cannot do, or have not achieved, we should spend time celebrating what it is we do offer. You may not be able to play the piano with the flair of Beethoven, but does your cooking make other people smile? And why waste time wishing you could sing like an angel, when your green thumb brings life to your garden?

None of this is to say that these things always come easily, or that hard work isn't involved. But it's all too easy to pine after something we haven't been able to master and forget all the wonderful things we have already achieved. So, celebrate your talents, whatever they are, big and small.

We don't have to
be good at everything.

SCYLLA & CHARYBDIS

Over the course of his ten-year journey from Troy to Ithaca, Odysseus faces many dangers, from irate gods to flesh-eating giants. One of the worst, however, is undoubtedly the combined might of Scylla and Charybdis.

The names Scylla and Charybdis are always mentioned in tandem in Homer's *Odyssey* for it is impossible to encounter one without the other. These two monsters sit on opposite sides of the Strait of Messina—a narrow passage of water that lies between Sicily and Calabria—waiting to prey on passing sailors (and dolphins).

According to Homer, Scylla is the daughter of a sea nymph named Crataeis. Unlike her mother, however, "she has twelve legs, six necks, and on each one a frightful head, and in it three rows of teeth, thick and close, full of black death." If the Roman poet Ovid is to be believed, their contrasting appearances are due to the fact that Scylla was once an ordinary nymph cursed by Circe to take on the appearance of a monster. However, this fact is not mentioned in the *Odyssey*.

Charybdis is even more difficult to describe. She is simply a monster; defined by her actions rather than her looks. From the rocks where she hides, she sucks down passing ships

→

"And in the midst of the cliff is a dim cave ... In it dwells Scylla, yelping terribly. Her voice to be sure is only as loud as the voice of a newborn whelp, but she herself is an evil monster, nor would anyone be glad at the sight of her, not even though it should be a god that met her.
[...]
But the other cliff, you will observe, Odysseus, is lower—they are close to each other; you could even shoot an arrow across—and on it is a large fig tree with rich foliage, but beneath this divine Charybdis sucks down the black water. Three times a day she belches it forth, and three times she sucks it down terribly. May you not be there when she sucks it down, for no one could save you from ruin, no, not the Earth-shaker." 12.80–109

"Scylla and Charybdis" has
become something of
a metaphor for navigating
tough decisions.

and sailors alike. Given this lack of physical description, it is probably no surprise that elsewhere she is simply depicted as a whirlpool with no body at all.

In summary, they are a duo you do not want to find yourself torn between, and yet this is exactly the position in which Odysseus and his men find themselves. As they prepare to set sail from Circe's island, the goddess warns them of what lies ahead. There is no avoiding the strait, and they—or rather Odysseus as their leader—must, therefore, make a difficult decision: to sail their ship past either Scylla or Charybdis. When faced with two such beasts this is a seemingly impossible choice.

Is it any wonder, then, that the story of Scylla and Charybdis has become something of a metaphor for navigating tough decisions. From the writings of Percy Shelley to Victor Hugo, you may well have come across allusions to Odysseus' conundrum before. On the one hand, our hero can steer toward Charybdis who will swallow his ship and crew whole. On the other, he can pass by Scylla who will reach out and grab as many men as possible. Of course, Circe advises him to take the second route: sacrificing a few lives, so that the rest might survive.

I hope that none of us ever face a situation quite like Odysseus', but I fear it is inevitable that we will all face dilemmas in our lives where neither option is ideal. In these situations, we need to assess the information we have and occasionally look for external advice. Only then can we properly weigh up both sides of a problem and decide which direction to take.

While we may be tempted to avoid making the decision altogether, when neither of the options seems ideal, there will be occasions in life when we simply must choose. The decision cannot be put off if you want to move forward. For Odysseus there was no other way to go around the Strait of Messina if he wanted to get home.

Making this decision likely won't be easy, but it is important. Otherwise, we might be left floating at sea, unable to get home.

LESSON EIGHTEEN

YOU CHOOSE YOUR FAMILY

"Did some kinsman of yours fall before Ilium,
some good, true man, your daughter's husband
or your wife's father, such as are nearest to one after
one's own kin and blood? Or was it perhaps some
[friend] dear to your heart, some good, true man?
For [a friend who understands] what is right
[is not inferior to a brother]."

8.584–86

During Odysseus' time in the Phaeacian kingdom, ruled over by the gracious Alcinous, the hero sits with his hosts and they are told a tale by one of their talented singers. The story he tells is that of the Trojan War. As his audience listens in, the singer recounts the loss of many men and women, some of whom were Odysseus' own friends and comrades. Neither the singer nor his king knows that one of the famed Greek soldiers sits before him. It is only when Alcinous looks over and sees his guest overcome with tears that he understands this tale hits close to home. Alcinous asks him about his connection to the war: did he lose a loved one, a family member, or even a friend?

While one takeaway from this scene could easily be a reminder to check in on those you see in distress, there is another point I want to draw your attention to. For Alcinous does not prioritize blood over the bonds of friendship. In fact, he states explicitly that a good friend or comrade is no less significant than a brother. Without knowing Odysseus' story, he appreciates that his grief might stem from the loss of any number of people he once knew, none more important than the other.

→

I believe this is an important reminder in a story about one's man struggle to be reunited with his family, that family can look like many things. Some family we are born to and some we find ourselves. The love we feel for those in our life, whether romantic or platonic, cannot be ranked and ordered. It is all, every drop of it, a part of our lives.

Friendship, meanwhile, is especially important when those you are expected to call family cannot provide you with the love and support you deserve. So, instead, we choose our own family and build something entirely new.

Evidently Homer was aware of the importance of found family. Thus, Alcinous reminds us to value every and all connections that plays a significant part in our lives. We all have the capacity to mean something to someone, and family comes in many forms.

A good friend or comrade
is no less significant
than a brother.

EUMAEUS & EURYCLEIA

Who are Eumaeus and Eurycleia, and why are they so often discussed in tandem? Eurycleia we meet first in Book One, accompanying Telemachus through the palace halls. She is an older woman, first brought to Ithaca by Odysseus' father Laertes. Apart from the fact she is the daughter of a man named Ops, son of Peisnor, we know nothing of her life before this. Over the years, however, she has served as wet-nurse to both Odysseus and Telemachus.

We know a little more about Eumaeus' background because he tells us himself. In Book Fifteen we learn that he was the son of Ctesius, king of Syra, essentially making him a prince. When he was still young, however, he was abducted by his own nurse when she in turn was seduced by a pirate. Yet this nurse was killed by Artemis and the pirate sold Eumaeus to Laertes. He was raised beside Odysseus and his sister Ctimene before taking over as the palace swineherd.

Both Eumaeus and Eurycleia were brought to Ithaca as young people. Both have watched Odysseus, then Telemachus, grow from boys to men. Both work in the royal household. Both are slaves.

All too often in discussions of Eumaeus and Eurycleia you will find them referred to as servants. However, this title only serves to sanitize the truth. They were purchased by Laertes; they had no choice in their position.

→

[Odysseus] found [Eumaeus] sitting in front of his house, where his court was built high in a place with a wide view, a beautiful great court with an open space around it. This the swineherd had himself built for the swine of his master that was gone, without the knowledge of his mistress and the old man Laertes. 14.5–9

Within the *Odyssey* and outside of it both figures are praised for their loyalty. When Odysseus returns to Ithaca Eumaeus gives him shelter and Eurycleia keeps his secret. They both assist him in various ways and are rewarded. In contrast with some of the other slaves in the palace they prove themselves worthy of Odysseus' generosity and compassion. Meanwhile, the king is quick to punish those slaves whose actions have displeased him, such as Penelope's attendants. These women he slaughters in cold blood for "colluding" with the suitors. His compassion is contingent.

And herein lies the issue with simply accepting the morals presented to us in ancient texts, or any text for that matter. They do not all hold value. Quite the opposite. This might sound counterintuitive given the premise of this very book. Yet, if anything, this is the context in which it is all the more important to emphasize this point. The exercise here is not simply to emulate the *Odyssey*, but rather to engage with the material on a deeper level.

Something that I touched on in my introduction is how we continuously find ourselves drawn to these ancient narratives. We are constantly in conversation with the many centuries of reception and interpretation they have received. That is what makes it all the more important to think critically about what we are reading. We should never blindly idolize the past; mythological characters or not, Eumaeus and Eurycleia deserve to be remembered for more than their service to Odysseus.

When [Eurycleia] had taken his leg in the flat of her hands [the old woman felt this scar and recognized it], and she let his leg fall. Into the basin his lower leg fell, and the bronze rang. It tipped over, and the water was spilled on the ground. Then upon her heart came joy and grief at the same moment, and her eyes were filled with tears and her voice caught in her throat. 19.467–72

Both figures are praised
for their loyalty.

LESSON NINETEEN

DON'T ASK OF OTHERS WHAT YOU WON'T DO YOURSELF

"I told the others to cast lots among them, which of them should have the hardihood with me to lift the stake and grind it into his eye when sweet sleep should come upon him. And the lot fell upon those whom I myself would have wished to choose; four they were, and I was numbered with them as the fifth."

9.331–35

Odysseus is not a perfect hero and Homer never implies as much. Yet among his many admirable qualities is the fact that he never asks of others what he will not do himself. During Book Nine of the *Odyssey*, Odysseus recounts his encounter with the Cyclops Polyphemus. He and his crew are trapped inside the giant's cave, desperate for a way to escape.

Of course, this is Odysseus we are speaking of, and it doesn't take long for the hero to come up with one of his quintessential clever plans. They will first blind the Cyclops and use his injury to hide beneath his flock of sheep in order to escape. In order to blind a giant such as Polyphemus, however, they need a weapon of equal size. One which requires a team of men to carry it.

Thus, Odysseus instructs his men to draw lots in order to decide who will wield the weapon; all but himself. From the moment that Odysseus devises his plan there is no doubt in his mind that he will lead the assault. He will put himself in equal, if not more, danger than the men he asks to trust him.

→

If there are tasks that must be done, Oydsseus will always contribute where he can.

In many ways, this is not the kind of king we find in other stories. The one who sits on his throne as he sends others to fight on his behalf. The one who rules from afar and never comes face to face with his people. Odysseus, on the other hand, does not consider himself above his men. If there are tasks that must be done, he will always contribute where he can.

It is an important lesson for us all to learn. Ideas are all well and good but without action they are nothing. Whether it's a team project (like defeating a Cyclops), or something even bigger like fighting for a better world, we should be willing to step up if we expect others to do the same. That doesn't mean everyone's contribution will always look the same (some tasks are a little more varied than wielding a giant spear). We all have different things to contribute, different skills and knowledge we can bring to the table. Yet, we should never leave all the labor to fall on others, especially if it's something we care about.

"Then I drew near and spoke to the Cyclops, holding in my hands an ivy-wood bowl of dark wine:

'Cyclops, here; drink wine, now that you have had your meal of human flesh, that you may know what kind of drink this is which our ship contained. It was to you that I was bringing it as a drink offering, in the hope that, touched with pity, you might send me on my way home; but you rage in a way that is past all bearing. Cruel man, how shall anyone of all the men there are ever come to you again hereafter, since what you have done is not right?'

So I spoke, and he took the cup and drained it, and was wondrously pleased as he drank the sweet draft, and asked me for it again a second time:

'Give me it again with a ready heart, and tell me your name at once, that I may give you a stranger's gift at which you may be glad.

For among the Cyclopes the earth, the giver of grain, bears the rich clusters of wine, and the rain of Zeus gives them increase; but this is a draft from a stream of ambrosia and nectar.'

So he spoke, and again I handed him the sparkling wine. Three times I brought and gave it to him, and three times he drained it in his folly. But when the wine had got round the wits of the Cyclops, then I spoke to him with winning words:

'Cyclops, you ask me of my glorious name, and I will tell you it; and do you give me a stranger's gift, even as you promised. Nobody is my name, Nobody they call me—my mother and my father, and all my comrades as well.'

So I spoke, and at once he answered me with pitiless heart: 'Nobody will I eat last among his comrades, and the others before him; this shall be your gift.'"

9.360–63

LESSON TWENTY

KNOW YOUR LIMITS

"Three times I brought and gave it to him,
and three times he drained it in his folly."

9.361–62

Before Odysseus and his men can blind Polyphemus and escape, they must incapacitate him. Thankfully, accomplishing this isn't exactly difficult. They simply need to get him drunk. While it is Odysseus and his men who offer Polyphemus their wine to drink, Homer is clear: it is the Cyclop's own greed and foolishness that leads to his downfall. For, as everyone knows, wine is better watered down.

Okay, so this doesn't necessarily apply to the bottles you'll find at the liquor store today. Modern wines typically come ready to drink, this is true. In ancient Greece, however, the fermented drink was incredibly strong; I always think of it more like modern spirits. This meant that it was standard practice to water down your drink and even add a few herbs and spices. There was no shame in enjoying a cup or two; the problems only started when people (and Cyclopes) drank in excess.

In essence, Homer tells us, know your limits.

And it's not just Homer who insists upon this. There are a number of ancient Greek texts that extol the virtue of learning when to say, "No thank you, I've had enough." One particularly

entertaining poem by the poet Eubulus opens with the line: "A sensible man may take three cups" before explaining what will come of every subsequent drink. A fifth will make the drinker talk nonsense, while the seventh will lead to fighting, and so on and so forth. The spirit of both texts remains the same.

For Polyphemus his excess spells his downfall. Yet, under other circumstances it is not just the drinker but those around them who are affected when things are taken too far. They become a burden and all the fun is quickly lost.

It's a takeaway that need not only apply to alcohol. Considering how our decisions affect those around us is something we could all take seriously. It's easy to get carried away with a joke or push ahead with a plan that isn't working out as we expected. Learning when to slow down, stop, and think, however, are invaluable skills regardless of the situation.

So, while we can thank the ancient Greeks for their contributions to vinification (wine making), we could probably also do well to remember the advice that goes along with it.

Learning when to slow down, stop, and think are invaluable skills.

THE UNDERWORLD
Looking Back to Go Forward

Welcome to the Underworld. Ruled over by the god Hades and goddess Persephone. The cost of entry is one obol to be paid to the ferryman Charon. Once you enter, though, you may never leave. Unless you're Odysseus, that is.

The ancient Greek Underworld's reputation precedes itself. Also known as Hades, this is the realm to which the souls of the dead descend. There is no equivalent of Heaven and Hell in ancient Greek religious belief; there is only the Underworld. Bad or good, everyone ends up in the same place.

However, there is a degree of stratification within the Underworld; it's not all one big soup of souls. Geographically the Underworld is said to be surrounded by rivers. In Homer's *Odyssey* these rivers remain uncounted and unnamed but later sources do identify five: the Styx, the Acheron, the Lethe, the Cocytus, and the Pyriphlegethon.

Beyond these rivers lies the Asphodel Fields. This location is named in the *Odyssey*, where it is described as the land in which the majority of the dead dwell. For those with a little more clout, however, there is Elysium. This portion of the Underworld is reserved for heroes and those favored by

→

"[Our ship] came to deep-flowing Oceanus, that bounds the Earth, where is the land and city of the Cimmerians, wrapped in mist and cloud. Never does the bright Sun look down on them with his rays either when he mounts the starry heaven or when he turns again to Earth from heaven, but instead horrid night is spread over wretched mortals. There we came and beached our ship, and took out the sheep, and ourselves went along beside the stream of Oceanus until we came to the place of which Circe had told us." 11.13–22

the gods. Before you assume these lines immovable, however, I should note that heroes such as Achilles and Patroclus explicitly appear in Homer's Asphodel Fields.

Finally, there is Tartarus. In some Ancient Greek sources Tartarus is simply another name for the Underworld, while in others it is a space reserved for punishing those individuals who have offended the gods. To further add to the confusion, the archaic poet Hesiod described Tartarus as a primordial being like Gaia and Ouranos. It is also never mentioned in the *Odyssey*.

All of this is to say: while the Underworld is a constant element of ancient Greek mythology and religious belief, its portrayal is not consistent. What is of interest to us here, therefore, is Homer's Underworld, and the role it plays in Odysseus' adventure.

In Book Ten of the *Odyssey*, we learn that Odysseus was sent to the Underworld by the goddess Circe. She told the hero that there he should speak to the now deceased seer Tiresias. This is how he will find his way back to Ithaca.

Even Odysseus' journey to the Underworld looks a little different from other ancient sources. Most notably, Homer never alludes to Odysseus traveling beneath the earth. Rather, the hero travels with his men across land and sea to a distant land that borders the entrance to the Underworld: the city of the Cimmerians. In this way, the path to the Underworld is no different from any other leg of his journey. Notably, the Cimmerians were a real nomadic people based in the Eurasian Steppe. Homer's city, meanwhile, appears only to take their name and nothing else.

When they arrive, Odysseus and his men must complete a series of complicated rituals laid out for them by Circe. First, they must find the spot where the river of fire and river of tears meet and dig a trench. Into the trench they should pour libations of honey, milk, and wine for the dead. Once this is complete Odysseus himself should sacrifice a ram and a ewe with his head turned away from the animals. Only then will the souls of the dead appear. And they do. In their thousands.

Also known as Hades, this is the realm to which the souls of the dead descend. There is no equivalent of Heaven and Hell in ancient Greek religious belief, there is only the Underworld. Bad or good, everyone ends up in the same place.

These ghosts, as it were, cannot speak until they drink the blood of the sacrificed beasts. So, one by one, Odysseus allows them to sup from the animals in order to speak to them as themselves. First is Elpenor, Odysseus' crewmate, who they have not realized died on Circe's island. Elpenor asks for a proper burial. Second is Odysseus' mother, Anticleia, but he delays his talk with her until he can speak to Tiresias who comes next.

As expected, Tiresias tells Odysseus of the many dangers he must yet encounter if he wishes to return to Ithaca, dangers we will learn about from Odysseus' own account. He also informs Odysseus that though he will eventually find his way home, he will have to make another journey afterward. This quest will require him to travel far and make sacrifices to Poseidon, but it is not recorded in the *Odyssey*.

After he learns what he needs to from the seer, Odysseus proceeds to speak with his mother, who tells him how his family are faring in his absence. He then speaks with Agamemnon, who tells the other king how he was murdered upon his return from Troy—a reminder for Odysseus to be cautious when he himself returns. Last but not least, he talks to Achilles, who insists that it is better to be alive but have nothing than to be a king among the dead.

All these encounters teach Odysseus something, whether practical or philosophical. He returns from the Underworld as a man who has processed his past and is better equipped to handle his future. It is not just a physical voyage he has taken but also a spiritual one. In this way, we are all capable of taking similar journeys simply through reflecting on what we have learned from our pasts, and who we wish to be in our futures. As Odysseus needs to confront what has gone before as part of his journey forward, we may also find it necessary to unpack elements of our past in order to create a happy future. Like a visit to the shady Underworld this may feel scary or unnerving, but you will inevitably reap the benefits. Our past has something to tell us, if we can put in the effort to uncover it.

LESSON TWENTY-ONE

BEWARE EXCESSIVE PRIDE

"So they spoke, but they could not persuade my great-hearted spirit; and I answered him again with angry heart: 'Cyclops, if any one of mortal men shall ask you about the shameful blinding of your eye, say that Odysseus, the sacker of cities, blinded it, the son of Laertes, whose home is in Ithaca.'"

9.500–05

Throughout the *Odyssey* we are privy to numerous examples of Odysseus' cleverness. He's a man with not just one plan but many, and he often uses his mind to get himself and his comrades out of sticky situations. And surely this is one of his great strengths and something we should all wish to emulate. Well, even Odysseus is fallible, as this moment perfectly encapsulates.

Perhaps one of Odysseus' most successful ideas is when he plots to blind the Cyclops Polyphemus in order for he and his crew to escape his man-eating clutches. And all goes exactly to plan. They get the Cyclops drunk, spear his singular eye while he sleeps, and stow away beneath his sheep when he lets them out to graze the next morning. The perfect escape. Perfect, that is, until Odysseus lets his success go to his head.

As the men sail away from Polyphemus' island, our hero shouts out at the top of his lungs, declaring that it was he, Odysseus, who blinded the Cyclops. Up until this point he had maintained his name was "Nobody." Emboldened by distance, however, Odysseus' pride undoes him. For whom is Polyphemus' father but the powerful sea god Poseidon? And now Poseidon knows his name.

Until now Poseidon has allowed Odysseus to travel relatively safely across the ocean on his journey home. But unsurprisingly the god does not take kindly to learning that this mortal man has harmed his son. Thus, it is this misstep

→

that places not just Odysseus, but also his men in the crosshairs of Poseidon for the rest of their miserable journey. If only Odysseus had kept his mouth shut.

To drive this point home further, Homer tells us that Odysseus' crewmates actually advised him against taunting the Cyclopes further. Somewhat desperately they beg him to not be so rash and enrage the mighty Cyclopes any further. Yet the hero ignores them. Is he not the clever one? The one who defeated the Cyclopes and saved their lives? Should he not claim his victory? Well, in doing exactly that he indirectly leads to their deaths through inciting Poseidon's ire.

Odysseus' actions might even be described as *hybris*, an Ancient Greek term that can refer to excessive pride and self-aggrandizement, often at the expense of others. *Hybris* was taken so seriously in Classical Athens that you could be tried and executed for it in court.

Of course, there is nothing wrong with taking pride in a job well done. What we're talking about here is pride in excess, and it is a good lesson to learn. Does your ego result in you treating others differently? In placing yourself on a pedestal do you forget that you too are fallible? This is when pride can harm both you and those around you. For Odysseus, the consequences are dire, but it is notable that he is more cautious from this moment on. He learns from his mistakes and so too can we.

There is nothing wrong with taking pride in a job well done. What we're talking about here is pride in excess, and it is a good lesson to learn.

MENELAUS

Throughout the *Odyssey*, a book positively obsessed with hospitality and guest friendship, Menelaus might just win the prize for being the ultimate host. Not only does he welcome Telemachus and Peisistratus into his home during the celebration of both his children's engagements, but when it is time for them to leave, he fills their hands with gifts, wishes them well, and even offers to accompany them. The most I've ever sent a dinner guest away with is leftovers.

With so much emphasis placed on hospitality in the *Odyssey*, however, it could be easy to overlook the significance of Menelaus' kindness. That is why it is so important to consider the king's actions in the context of broader mythological events, context that ancient Greek readers would undoubtedly have had. For, if anyone should be suspicious of uninvited guests, it is Menelaus.

Son of the Mycenaean king Atreus and his wife Aerope, Menelaus lost out on his father's throne to his brother Agamemnon. Luckily for him, however, there were plenty of thrones to go around and he set out to find a wife through whom he might inherit one. Enter Helen. When the Spartan princess came of age, Menelaus traveled to her father's kingdom to request her hand in marriage. Unfortunately for him, he wasn't the only one.

→

Then Peisistratus, son of Nestor, answered, and said: "Telemachus, in no way can we drive through the dark night, however eager for our journey; and soon it will be dawn. Wait then, until the hero son of Atreus, Menelaus, famed for his spear, shall bring gifts and set them on the chariot, and shall send us on our way with kindly words of farewell. For a guest remembers all his days the host who shows him kindness." 15.46–55

Tyndareus, Helen's stepfather and king of Sparta, had his pick of suitors. Too many, in fact. He feared the suitors might turn on one another, so he asked Odysseus, famed for his intelligence, for assistance and the king of Ithaca suggested a pact. The men would hold a contest for Helen's hand and whoever did not win would swear to protect the winner's marriage. Who won? Menelaus, of course.

So, Menelaus and Helen were wed, and Menelaus became king of Sparta through his wife. It could have been their happy ever after if they hadn't allowed another man to stay in their home: Paris.

When the Trojan prince Paris was promised Helen's hand in marriage as a reward by Aphrodite, the goddess didn't care one ounce that Helen was already married. No, Paris is sent to Sparta where Menelaus welcomes him with open arms and extends him the hand of guest friendship, or *xenia*. When Menelaus is called away for a funeral, however, Paris abducts Helen, effectively throwing Menelaus' hospitality in his face. This is the catalyst for the Trojan War. The Greek leaders who fought for Helen's hand band together to retrieve Menelaus' wife from Troy. Oh, and his claim to the Spartan throne ... In reality, their motives are a little too complicated to distill into this brief profile.

Why I find this so interesting in the context of the *Odyssey*, however, is that Menelaus does not appear to have come away jaded from this experience with Paris. Despite what happened almost twenty years ago—and led to a decade-long war—he has not abandoned the values of *xenia*.

Throughout his encounter with Telemachus and Peisistratus, Menelaus goes above and beyond for the two young men. More importantly, perhaps, is that he does so before he even knows who they are. The two are already settled around his dining table when Helen asks if Telemachus is the son of Odysseus—she immediately sees the family resemblance. Menelaus, meanwhile, simply sees two travelers in need of a meal and a place to lay their head.

Some might call him foolish or chide him for not "learning his lesson." I, however, see a man who does not take his values lightly. One bad experience does not lead Menelaus to abandon all that he has built his life around. To him, his commitment to hospitality is equally his honor as a Greek. Paris may have taken his kindness for granted, may have trampled on the friendship he offered, but that doesn't mean he gets to take Menelaus' values from him too.

I also don't think it matters that Telemachus and Peisistratus are more trustworthy guests. Menelaus invited both men to be his guests without any prior knowledge of who they were, albeit he recognized them as the sons of kings. In offering them the comforts of his home he was simply behaving in a way he considered honorable. Is there not something rather admirable in such a commitment to what matters most to you, regardless of whether others do the same?

One bad experience does not lead Menelaus to abandon all that he has built his life around.

LESSON TWENTY-TWO

HONOR THE DEAD

"[I] poured a libation to all the dead, first with milk and honey, thereafter with sweet wine, and in the third place with water, and I sprinkled on it white barley meal and I earnestly entreated the strengthless heads of the dead, vowing that when I came to Ithaca I would sacrifice in my halls a barren heifer, the best I had, and load the altar with rich gifts, and to Tiresias alone would sacrifice a ram, wholly black, the finest of my flocks."

11.26–34

For the characters of Homeric poetry, honoring the dead isn't just "a nice thing to do"—it is a religious obligation. When Odysseus arrives in the Underworld in search of answers, he vows to make sacrifices in their honor once he is restored to his kingdom. This is not simply about taking what he can from the dead but recognizing their contribution to his journey.

For Odysseus this contribution is obviously quite literal. The souls of his departed friends and relatives share with him what they know of both the past and present—it was commonly believed in ancient Greece that the dead can see into the future—and he is able to use this knowledge in his quest. It's only natural, therefore, that the hero might feel indebted to them. As modern readers, meanwhile, there remains a symbolic truth to Homer's poem. For this is what honoring the dead is all about.

Just as Odysseus completes the above ritual, he is approached by the soul of his companion Elpenor. Unbeknownst to Odysseus, Elpenor fell to his death when walking along the roof of Circe's home. He asks the hero to bury him upon his return to Ithaca and place an oar in the soil

as a grave marker. This symbol will bestow on Elpenor the honor of being remembered as a member of Odysseus' crew. Of course, Odysseus does exactly this.

In many ways Elpenor's character contrasts with that of Odysseus. Unlike the hero, he is irresponsible and his blunder means he will never return home. Nevertheless, this doesn't mean that he is undeserving of receiving the honors due to the dead or being remembered.

For the ancient Greeks these honors took many forms: from private and public funerary rites, depending on the city-state, to continual commemoration through libations and festivals for the dead. Funerals for high-status individuals like royalty might feature athletic games such as those featured in Homer's *Iliad*, while democratic Athens hosted publicly funded funerals for the city's war dead.

Throughout history the way in which we honor the dead looks different for different people, whether guided by cultural, familial, or religious traditions. You might not even realize when you're doing it. It might look like sharing a memory or visiting a loved one's favorite spot. Whatever it is, we all do it, and Homer thinks that matters. In honoring the dead, we keep their memories alive; it acknowledges the impact they had and the parts of us that were made by them.

This is about recognizing the dead's contribution to his journey.

ARGOS

Of all the figures in the *Odyssey* who I've written about for this volume, Argos is undoubtedly the one with the fewest lines in the poem itself. Yet, somehow, this character, who never speaks, and who dies within minutes of appearing on the page, and who just so happens to be a dog, has inextricably impressed himself upon the popular memory of this millennia-old epic.

Argos is everywhere. Beyond written accounts of Odysseus' adventures, you can find him on silver Roman coins from the first century CE. One example shows Odysseus accompanied by Argos on the reverse side of a coin that also depicts the god Hermes. These are the same coins that in other instances might feature the faces of important political figures such as emperors and empresses. Yet here they are adorned with a mythological canine.

More recently, Argos has taken center stage in the work of eighteenth-century Italian artist Giovanni Battista Tiepolo, while the American writer James Baldwin retold his tale in his 1905 short story collection *Thirty More Famous Stories Retold*. Over the course of 3,000 years this simple dog has traveled the globe and found a place in countless hearts. That has to mean something, doesn't it?

→

And a dog that lay there raised his head and pricked up his ears, Argos, steadfast Odysseus' dog, whom of old he had himself bred ... In days past the young men were accustomed to take the dog to hunt the wild goats, and deer, and hares; but now he lay neglected, his master gone, in the deep dung of mules and cattle, which lay in heaps before the doors ... There lay the dog Argos, full of dog ticks. But now, when he became aware that Odysseus was near, he wagged his tail and dropped both ears, but nearer to his master he had no longer strength to move. Then Odysseus looked aside and wiped away a tear. 17.290–304

Argos reminds us of our own relationship with our beloved pets.

In the *Odyssey* we meet Argos for the first and last time in Book Seventeen. We are alerted to his presence when he recognizes a familiar voice and pricks up his ears. The voice, of course, is that of his old master Odysseus. Argos had been reared and trained by Odysseus as a puppy and served as a companion to his master when he went hunting. They were only separated when the king was called upon to fight in the Trojan War some twenty years earlier.

Even after all this time, Argos recognizes Odysseus. Odysseus' disguise as a beggar, which has fooled everyone else so convincingly, is no match for his four-legged friend. In fact, Argos is the only character to recognize Odysseus so quickly. He is old, however, and upon learning his master has finally returned home Argos takes his last breath.

It is a tragic tale in some regards, one that emphasizes the length of time Odysseus has been absent, and what that time has taken from him. Homer's characterization of Argos is by no means divorced from reality; it is well established that dogs have long memories. They are also incredibly clever, something Homer evidently recognized. They remember those who were kind to them and those who treated them poorly.

Perhaps one of the reasons that we as modern readers are still so captivated by Argos, therefore, is that he reminds us of our own relationship with our beloved pets. Argos remembers the love and affection Odysseus had showed him decades before and he is no exception. How dogs, and other animals, respond to us is a result of how we treat them. Whether they live in our homes or not we owe it to our fellow creatures to treat them with kindness and compassion. This is not a modern idea, but an ancient one.

LESSON TWENTY-THREE

PRACTICE PATIENCE

"My honored mother answered without delay:
'Only too truly she remains with steadfast heart
in your halls, and ever sorrowfully for her do
the nights and days wane, as she weeps.'"

11.180–84

During his visit to the Underworld Odysseus is reunited with a great many departed souls, including his mother, Anticleia. The hero is distraught to learn that in the thirteen years since he last laid eyes on her, his mother has passed away from grief when he did not return from Troy. Naturally this only makes him all the more desperate to learn of what has befallen the rest of his family in Ithaca. He asks after his father and son—curious if they have retained his inheritance—as well as his wife, wondering if she has waited for him all this time or found another husband in his absence.

As readers, we are well aware by this point that Penelope has long hoped for the return of her husband, but we must not forget that this is the first time Odysseus has had news of his family. To his relief, Anticleia informs him that he need not worry. Should he return home he will find his wife waiting for him, for if Penelope is one thing, she is patient.

Penelope's steadfast nature is praised not just in Homer's *Odyssey* but in later Greek literature as well. She is a role model who has inspired others for millennia at this point and rightly so. Nor is it only in the years spent waiting for Odysseus' return that we see her patience exemplified.

→

When Odysseus finally reveals himself to his wife in Book Twenty-three of Homer's poem, Penelope does not immediately accept his identity. Not unlike her husband has done to others, she tests him. She instructs Eurycleia to have her marital bed brought to the great hall, so that she and the man who claims to be Odysseus might lie together. Theirs is no ordinary bed, though. It was carved by Odysseus himself from a tree that remains rooted to the ground, thus making the bed immovable. A fact that only Penelope and the real Odysseus know. When Odysseus objects, therefore, his identity is confirmed.

The two really are a perfect fit, for patience is a virtue Odysseus shares with his wife. We witness this on the numerous occasions he holds back his true identity until he is sure it is safe to do so. Penelope's patience, meanwhile, is neither inactive nor pointless. Her patience has purpose; she does not wait for nothing.

It's a simple lesson but no less important for it. Rather than making assumptions or rushing into situations without any more information, taking a pause and assessing a situation can often lead to much better results. Indeed, some of the greatest things in life take time. You can plant the seeds and tend the soil, but then you might just need to sit back and wait a little for your work to come to fruition. In other words, give it time. You never know what might happen.

Penelope's steadfast nature is praised not just in Homer's *Odyssey* but in later Greek literature as well.

"Stubborn men, who have gone down alive to the house of Hades to meet death twice, while other men die but once. But come, eat food and drink wine here this whole day through; but at the coming of dawn you shall set sail, and I will point out the way and declare to you each thing, in order that through wretched ill-contriving you may not suffer pain and woes either by sea or on land."

So she spoke, and our proud hearts consented. So then all day long till sunset we sat feasting on abundant meat and sweet wine. But when the Sun set and darkness came on, they lay down to rest beside the stern cables of the ship; but Circe took me by the hand, and leading me apart from my staunch comrades, made me sit, and lay down beside me and asked me all the tale. And I told her all in due order. Then queenly Circe spoke to me and said:

"So did all that come to pass"; and "Now listen to what I shall tell you, and a god shall himself bring it to your mind. First you will come to the Sirens, who beguile all men who come to them. Whoever in ignorance draws near to them and hears the Sirens' voice, his wife and little children never stand beside him and rejoice at his homecoming; instead, the Sirens beguile him with their clear-toned song, as they sit in a meadow, and about them is a great heap of bones of moldering men, and round the bones the skin is shriveling. But row past them, and anoint the ears of your comrades with sweet wax, which you have kneaded, for fear any of the rest may hear. But if you yourself have a will to listen, let them bind you in the swift ship hand and foot upright in the step of the mast, and let the ropes be made fast at the ends to the mast itself, that with delight you may listen to the voice of the two Sirens. And if you shall implore and command your comrades to free you, then let them bind you with yet more bonds."

12.21–47

LESSON TWENTY-FOUR

LISTEN TO GOOD ADVICE

"Now listen to what I shall tell you,
and a god shall himself bring it to your mind."
12.37–38

Possibly one of Odysseus' most famous feats is his clever escape from the deadly Sirens. These mythical creatures—half-woman, half-bird—lure sailors to their death with just their singing voice. You've probably even heard the descriptor "siren's song" to refer to something alluring and dangerous. Well, according to Greek mythology Odysseus is one of the only humans to have heard this song and survived—all thanks to the goddess Circe.

Though Odysseus is certainly intelligent and cunning in his own right, he doesn't know everything. Often his intelligence is shown through his capacity to heed good advice. He does not bristle at the idea another might know more than him. Rather, he listens to what others have to say and uses this information to his best ability.

In the case of the Sirens, Odysseus does exactly as Circe instructs. He commands his men to stuff their ears full of wax, so that they might not be tempted by the Sirens' call. Meanwhile, he is strapped to the mast and prevented from following the deadly song even as he listens. It's a good plan. And while Circe deserves credit for suggesting it, Odysseus should also be recognized for implementing it.

Nor is this the only time we see Odysseus taking advice from others that directly contributes to his success. Athena, for example, is a constant source of advice for our hero. He also takes advice from Nausicaa on how best to approach her parents, and the sea goddess Leucothea when she tells him to abandon his raft and swim. In fact, Odysseus' ability to take advice and knowledge from those he encounters is a consistent theme throughout Homer's poem. While his many stops on the way home cause him to be repeatedly delayed, there are very few episodes during his quest where he doesn't learn something from someone he meets. If we simply open our minds, then our lives can be the same.

Too often we convince ourselves that a victory is only worthwhile if we win it by ourselves. Yet it is truly impossible to know everything. No one person can carry the weight of all knowledge (even in Greek mythology). Like Odysseus, therefore, we must be open to what others can teach us. If Odysseus had ignored Circe, he would surely have been just another of the ignorant men she describes; the ones lost at sea who are never able to return home.

Often Odysseus' intelligence is shown through his capacity to heed good advice.

LESSON TWENTY-FIVE

HAVE FAITH IN YOURSELF

"Friends, hitherto we have been not at all ignorant of sorrow; surely this evil that besets us now is no greater than when the Cyclops penned us in his hollow cave by brutal strength; yet even from there we made our escape through my valor and counsel and wit; these dangers, too, I think, we shall someday remember."

12.208–11

Odysseus is brave. Odysseus is strong. Odysseus is clever. And he knows it. At this point in the *Odyssey*, he has escaped a goddess, traveled to the Underworld, defeated a Cyclops, and generally done a lot of really impressive stuff. With the help of his crew, of course. Thus, it is not without good reason that he reminds his men what they are capable of when their confidence begins to wane.

At this, almost precisely the midway point of the poem, Odysseus and his men have managed to avoid being lured in by the Sirens' song, thanks to Circe's advice, only to be ambushed by the unruly ocean. The waves are coming thick and fast, and in their terror the sailors temporarily drop their oars, so their ship is simply floating aimlessly atop the water. This is the moment Odysseus gives his rousing speech.

In contrast with the brash pride Odysseus displays during Book Nine—when he irresponsibly taunts Polyphemus with his real name—his actions in this scene rally his comrades and guide them through the fog of fear. He doesn't bluster. What

→

he says is true. These are brave men who have accomplished much and there is nothing wrong with acknowledging that. He asks them: What's a little turbulence to men who have already come this far? Have a little faith. In whom? Yourself.

And while we might not have an Odysseus to tell us so, we could certainly all do with remembering this too. Recognizing what you have achieved in the past and are capable of in the future might not always come easily, but that's what makes it so important. You might not think it, but you have come a long way. We all have. You are here now and there is so much more ahead of you. You just need to believe.

When Odysseus tells his men, "These dangers, too, I think, we shall someday remember," he reminds them that they have encountered trouble before and come through it, but he also asks them to envisage a future when they will look back at this difficult time as simply a memory. It is a powerful message, reminding us perhaps of the adage: "This too shall pass."

In other words, pick up those metaphorical oars, keep on rowing, and have confidence in yourself to pull through. One day, these difficulties will be behind us.

Have a little faith.
In whom?
Yourself.

But Pallas Athene went to spacious Lacedaemon to remind the glorious son of great-hearted Odysseus of his return, and to hasten his coming. She found Telemachus and the noble son of Nestor lying in the porch of the palace of glorious Menelaus. Now Nestor's son was overcome with soft sleep, but sweet sleep did not hold Telemachus, but all through the immortal night anxious thoughts for his father kept him wakeful. And flashing-eyed Athene stood near him, and said:

"Telemachus, you do not do well to wander longer far from your home, leaving behind you your wealth and men in your house so insolent; beware lest they divide and devour all your possessions, and you shall have gone on a fruitless journey. Instead, rouse with all speed Menelaus, good at the war cry, to send you on your way, that you may find your flawless mother still in her home. For now, her father and her brothers press her to marry Eurymachus, for he surpasses all the suitors in his presents, and has increased the gifts of wooing. Beware lest she carry from your halls some treasure against your will. For you know what sort of a spirit there is in a woman's breast; she wishes to increase the house of the man who marries her, but of her former children and staunch spouse she takes no thought, when once he is dead, and asks no longer concerning them.

[...]

So saying, she departed to high Olympus. But Telemachus woke the son of Nestor out of sweet sleep, rousing him with a touch of his heel, and spoke to him, saying:

"Awake, Peisistratus, son of Nestor; bring up your solid-hoofed horses, and yoke them beneath the chariot, that we may speed on our way."

15.1–47

LESSON TWENTY-SIX

DON'T DELAY

Pallas Athene went to spacious Lacedaemon
to remind the glorious son of great-hearted
Odysseus of his return, and to hasten his coming.

15.1–2

With Odysseus' return to Ithaca in Book Thirteen, it is now time for Telemachus to come home—or so says Athena at least. The goddess comes to Telemachus during the night, while he lies restlessly beside the sleeping Peisistratus. Through his fog of exhaustion, the prince listens to Athena as she instructs him to reboard his ship and journey back to Ithaca. There's no time to linger.

But why the sudden rush? Athena does not tell Telemachus that Odysseus has returned, but she does inform him that should he stay away any longer, he might lose just about everything. The suitors are growing bolder by the day, wasting the prince's inheritance bit by bit. Meanwhile, his mother, Penelope, faces increasing pressure to marry the suitor known as Eurymachus. He has showered her father and brothers with gifts and now they think it is time she gave up on Odysseus once and for all.

By all accounts, should Telemachus wait too long, he'll return to an empty home—with his belongings and his mother long gone from its halls. We as readers, meanwhile, also know that Eurymachus is plotting Telemachus' death, though Athena doesn't share this detail.

It is a useful skill to
recognize when an occasion
calls for haste.

I like to think that if we delay a little, we—you and I—won't typically run the risk of an assassination attempt, but it certainly is a useful skill to recognize when an occasion calls for haste. There will likely be times in all our lives when we need to put distractions to one side and step on it. For Telemachus this was one such situation.

After his visit from Athena, Telemachus wakes Peisistratus and plans their journey home. Though Menelaus offers to escort the two, Telemachus declines the offer because this would only slow them down. And even when he delivers Peisistratus to his own kingdom, he avoids visiting his friend's father's palace lest he be waylaid.

It is important to note, however, that Athena does not rebuke Telemachus for leaving home in the first place. It was she who advised him to visit Nestor and Menelaus in order to learn more about his father after all. She is simply reminding him that it is now time to move on.

As we have discussed elsewhere in this book, the *Odyssey* is a poem that encourages taking time to rest and think. It never suggests that its heroes rush into situations unprepared. Once this time has passed, however, comes the time to act. Time to take what you have learned and put it into practice.

LESSON TWENTY-SEVEN

BE ADAPTABLE

"In all truth I was about to have perished in my halls by the evil fate of Agamemnon, son of Atreus, had you not, goddess, duly told me all. But come, weave some plan by which I may requite them; and stand by my side yourself, and imbue me with dauntless courage, as when we loosed the bright diadem of Troy. Would you but stand by my side, you of the flashing eyes, as eager as you were then, I would fight even against three hundred men, with you, mighty goddess, if with a ready heart you would give me aid."

13.382–91

For all that the *Odyssey* is most often associated with Odysseus' time at sea, the hero actually returns to Ithaca's shores only a little more than halfway through the epic. Thirteen books in and finally his struggles are over. What could possibly fill the rest of those pages? Unfortunately, unlike Odysseus, we know what awaits him in his palace—and it's not just his wife and son. Unwelcome suitors fill his halls, enjoying his wealth, competing for his wife, and hoping against hope the king never returns.

Fortunately for Odysseus, he does have a friend who knows what's what: Athena. When the hero washes ashore the goddess meets him on the sand and tells him what has happened in Ithaca in his absence.

As far as Odysseus was concerned, his quest was over; he had braved the dangerous journey and all the monsters along the way. Now, he can go home and be reunited with the ones he loves. Except, following Athena's news, he no longer knows who to trust or whether he will survive the mere act of showing up on his own doorstep. As he says, he may well have been about to walk into his own murder, like Agamemnon in Mycenae.

So, Odysseus is forced to rethink his existing plan. He allows the goddess to transform his appearance and pretends he is a beggar. Thanks to this disguise, he is able to slowly introduce himself to the comings and goings of Ithaca once more, to test those he knew previously, and confirm who remains loyal before challenging the suitors. It is a plan that works out very well indeed.

This is what Odysseus gets for being adaptable. He defeats the suitors, is restored to his family, and reclaims his kingdom. When he realizes that his original plan isn't going to do the trick, he doesn't allow himself to become bogged down or frustrated. He accepts the situation, it is what it is, and then pivots and goes in another direction.

Inevitably, we will all find ourselves in Odysseus' position. Not washed ashore on a Greek island after a decade at sea, but discovering that the road we had outlined for ourselves is blocked by some obstacle or another. Rather than stubbornly beating our heads against the metaphorical wall, however, sometimes the best thing to do is pick ourselves up and consider a new path instead.

Odysseus is forced to
rethink his existing plan.

ZEUS

Meet Zeus. Ruler on Olympus. King of the Gods. And the baby of the family. Yes, that's right. Of six divine siblings Zeus was, in fact, the youngest. So, how did he come to be in charge? Well, it's a classic story really ...

Zeus was the son of the Titans Kronos and Rhea. At this point in ancient Greek mythology, Kronos was king among the gods and feared being usurped by his children—probably because he'd done exactly that to his own father, Ouranos. Kronos' strategy? Eat any children he and Rhea conceived while they were still babies.

Except Rhea didn't much care for this plan. So, when she was pregnant with Zeus, she decided to trick her husband. When the time came for her to give birth, she did so in hiding. Then, rather than hand over baby Zeus to Kronos, she wrapped a giant rock in blankets and gave it to his father. Kronos, never having had any reason to question his wife before, swallowed the bundle without checking what was inside.

Rhea went on to raise Zeus in secret, preparing him to one day overthrow his father. When the time came, Zeus disguised himself as servant and gave Kronos a poisoned cup. The contents caused the Titan to throw up all five of Zeus' older siblings: Demeter, Hera, Hestia, Hades, and Poseidon.

→

"Father Zeus, who are lord over gods and men, how loudly you have thundered from the starry sky, yet nowhere is there any cloud: surely this is a sign which you are showing to someone. Fulfill now even for me the word that I shall speak. May the suitors this day for the last and latest time hold their glad feast in the halls of Odysseus. They who have loosened my limbs with bitter labor, as I made them barley meal, may they now sup their last."

So [the mill woman] spoke, and noble Odysseus was glad at the word of omen and at the thunder of Zeus, for he thought to take vengeance on the guilty.

20.112–21

Led by Zeus, the siblings, who became known as the Olympians, gathered together as many gods and goddesses as they could, and led a war against Kronos and his supporters. Of course, they eventually won, and the time came to divide leadership over the world between them. Demeter had agriculture, Hera had marriage, and Hestia had the home, but there remained the seas, the Underworld, and the earth and sky.

In order to decide who would rule over each realm the three men decided to draw straws. Hades drew the short straw and became god of the Underworld. Poseidon drew next and was awarded the oceans. While Zeus, who pulled the final straw, became king of the earth and skies.

Zeus went on to rule over his domains from Mount Olympus where he also served as the ultimate judge among the gods. For Zeus, like his fellow deities, is the god of many things. Thunder, lightning, justice, freedom, hospitality; the list goes on. It is in his role as god of justice that he plays a particularly significant role in the *Odyssey*.

During Homer's epic, Zeus never interacts with Odysseus or the other mortals directly. Rather, he acts as arbitrator among the deities, always making the final decision on what they should or should not do. Luckily for Odysseus, that's usually in his favor.

Two of Zeus' major contributions to the narrative bookend the poem. We first encounter him in Book One when Athena goes to him to petition for Odysseus' return home. Zeus listens to his daughter, though he must also consider his brother Poseidon's anger toward the man who blinded his son. In the end he weighs up the relevant factors and decides to support Athena. As he sees it, Odysseus has already suffered enough, while Poseidon must learn when to let go of his anger.

Then we come to the end of the poem, when the people of Ithaca storm Laertes' home seeking vengeance for Odysseus' slaughter of the suitors. Once again, Athena goes to Zeus to ask him what should happen now. Zeus decrees that the time has come for the mortals to put down their weapons and live in peace. There has been enough bloodshed, and this is where it needs to end—a message Athena happily delivers.

As previously mentioned, Odysseus generally benefits from Zeus' decisions in the *Odyssey*. Though it is worth noting that the king of the gods is also not averse to delivering punishments in the poem. When Odysseus' men ignore his warnings and sacrifice the cattle of Helios, it is Zeus who strikes down their ship, killing all of the hero's crew and stranding him on Calypso's Island, the same place we find him when Zeus decides he has finally suffered enough. While this punishment might seem extreme, we have to bear in mind that the sailors had fair warning. After all, Tiresias told them that harming the cattle would offend the gods.

Elsewhere in Greek mythology Zeus is certainly no bastion of virtue. He can be fickle and capricious, and he might be the perfect example of "Do as I say, not as I do." Within the *Odyssey*, however, he represents justice. He listens carefully and considers the thoughts of others. And though it would be the ancient equivalent of blasphemy to claim to be on a par with Zeus himself, I don't think there's anything wrong with channeling a bit of this energy in our own mortal lives.

Once again, Athena goes to Zeus to ask him what should happen now. Zeus decrees that the time has come for the mortals to put down their weapons and live in peace. There has been enough bloodshed, and this is where it needs to end—a message Athena happily delivers.

LESSON TWENTY-EIGHT

HEROES SHARE

"God-touched man, I harm you not in deed or word, nor do I begrudge that any man should give to you, even if the portion he took up should be a large one. This threshold will hold us both, and you have no need to be jealous of what others get. You seem to be a vagrant like me; and as for prosperity, it is to the gods we must look for that."

18.15–22

In some ways Book Eighteen of the *Odyssey* opens with a pause in the action. Odysseus has reached Ithaca. He has revealed himself to his loyal servant and his son. Together they have hatched a plan to oust Penelope's suitors and take back the hero's home. Before this final episode unfolds, however, Odysseus, in his disguise as a beggar, encounters a man named Irus whose ill reputation precedes him.

Irus is arrogant, self-serving, and greedy. He serves the suitors and, most importantly here, refuses to share what he has. Upon finding Odysseus on the steps of the palace, Irus threatens to fight him should he not get off— this is *his* place of rest, doesn't he know?

In this moment, Irus is the antithesis of our hero. For Odysseus' response, as we see in the quote opposite could not be more different. He argues that they can easily share the threshold. There is no need to fight, for why should one man hold onto more than he needs when there is enough for two? Irus doesn't agree, of course, but Irus isn't the character with whom the reader is supposed to side; something which is cemented by Odysseus' quick defeat of the other man when he insists on fighting over the threshold.

Nor is it inconsequential that Odysseus chooses this moment to impart these words of wisdom. Throughout the *Odyssey* we have seen both how greed corrupts and how important it is to share what we have. Yet in this scene, it is not great piles of wealth at stake, but simply a roof over one's head and a place to rest.

Even when what he has seems small, Odysseus reminds us of how important it is to share with others. It is also significant that Irus is not purely spurred on by his own greed, but the suitors specifically goad him to fight this stranger for what is little more than a covered stoop, the same suitors who gorge on rich food and sleep in fine beds. These men convince Irus that he must fight another man for the little they give him rather than demand more for his work in the first place.

The *Odyssey* therefore tells us that there is more than enough to go around; we simply need to share.

Why should one man hold
onto more than he needs when
there is enough for two?

ODYSSEUS

Oh, Odysseus. The man, the myth, the legend. Where does one begin to summarize the man who gives the *Odyssey* its very title? I suppose I'll need to start at the beginning.

Odysseus was the son of Laertes and Anticleia, the king and queen of Ithaca; he also had a younger sister named Ctimene who we never hear much about. That is about as much as we know of Odysseus' early years. He only really becomes a prominent part of ancient mythology during the contest for Helen's hand. This is also when we are treated to the first example of the cleverness for which he becomes known. For, when the men of Greece look set to turn on each other if they themselves do not get to marry Helen, Odysseus devises a plan. All of Helen's suitors should swear an oath that no matter who her father chooses, they will defend the marriage against any who threaten it. For his efforts, Helen's father arranges the marriage of Odysseus to his niece Penelope.

The problem is that when Helen is abducted by the Trojan prince Paris, Odysseus is also called on to fight alongside her husband, something he really doesn't want to do. Not because he is a coward or incapable of joining the battle. Rather, he has been informed of a prophecy that says if he goes to Troy he will experience a long-delayed journey home. Prophetic indeed.

→

With an angry glance from beneath his brows resourceful Odysseus answered them: "You dogs, you thought that I should never again come home from the land of the Trojans, seeing that you wasted my house, and lay with the maid servants by force, and while I was still alive covertly courted my wife, having no fear of the gods, who hold broad heaven, or that any indignation of men would follow. Now over you one and all have the cords of destruction been made fast." 22.34–42

So Odysseus comes up with another plan. He's going to pretend to have lost his mind. There are a few different versions of how he does this. In one he yokes a donkey and ox to his plow and begins to sow his fields with salt. In another he simply pretends to rant and rave when Prince Palamedes comes to fetch him for war. Either way, Palamedes doesn't believe it, and he uses Odysseus' newborn son Telemachus to prove it. In scenario one he places the baby in the path of the plow, while in scenario two he brings his own sword to the baby's throat. Both actions force Odysseus to snap out of his pretense and run to his son's aid, thus proving Palamedes' theory and forcing Odysseus to join the Greek army.

It is fortunate for the Greeks that Odysseus is with them because after ten long years of fighting, it is his idea that saves them. Yes, I'm speaking of the Trojan horse. Instructed by Odysseus, the Greeks build a giant horse made of wood and leave it as a supposed offering to Athena outside the gates of Troy. Of course, as you may already know, the horse turns out to be hollow and filled to the brim with warriors, including Odysseus himself. The rest of the Greeks make themselves scarce and the Trojans, thinking they have given up, bring the magnificent structure inside their city walls. A decision that proves to be their downfall when the Greek soldiers reveal themselves and take the Trojans unawares.

The rest of Odysseus' story is recounted in the *Odyssey* itself. Between the main narrative and the hero's flashbacks we hear of the many dangerous encounters that have waylaid him, as well as how he overcame them. From his escape from the Cyclops Polyphemus to his defeat of his wife Penelope's suitors, we learn of the ways in which Odysseus used his mind to solve his problems, just as he was known for doing before the events of Homer's epic.

Odysseus is the perfect example that you don't have to be the biggest or brawniest to win the battle—whether that battle be literal or figurative. The reason he was celebrated in antiquity, and we still remember him today, is his sharp mind and cunning.

Odysseus is the perfect example that you don't have to be the biggest or brawniest to win the battle—whether that battle be literal or figurative. The reason he was celebrated in antiquity, and we still remember him today, is his sharp mind and cunning. When Homer asks the Muse to tell them Odysseus' story, they refer to him as *polytropon*, a word that has been translated variously as "of many devices" (Murray), "complicated" (Wilson), or "resourceful" (Rieu), to name a few. "Wily" is another good option. All of which are correct, for Odysseus is all of these things.

Odysseus' mind is also what won him the favor of the gods themselves. Athena describes her heart as torn for the wise man who has suffered so much. Likewise, Zeus agrees that Odysseus, wiser than all other mortals, has sacrificed enough—so they help him. They help him because they see in him qualities that they admire: cunning, intelligence, resourcefulness. So much so that they even refer to him as *theioio* or godlike. In Odysseus they see a little of themselves.

None of this is to say that Odysseus is perfect. For all his successful plans we also see him fail. Nor is this a criticism. If anything, it makes the king more relatable. If even the great hero Odysseus can mess things up and still receive thousands of years' worth of praise, maybe we can be a little bit kinder to ourselves when we also make mistakes. What matters is that we are able to reflect on what went wrong and learn from it. This is what true intelligence looks like. This is what Odysseus exemplifies.

LESSON TWENTY-NINE

DON'T STAND BY WHILE OTHERS SUFFER

"What a thing is this that has been done in these halls, that you have let this stranger be so maltreated! How would it be if the stranger, while sitting as he does in our house, should come to some harm through being roughly dragged about? On you, then, would fall shame and disgrace among men."

18.219–24

When Telemachus is finally reunited with his father in Ithaca, the two quickly hatch a plan to eliminate his mother's unwelcome suitors. This scheme requires Odysseus to remain in disguise as a beggar, hiding his true identity from everyone in the palace, including Penelope. Thus, when Penelope first sees her long-lost husband again, she has no idea who he is—whether she truly remains in the dark until he later reveals himself is a question much debated by scholars.

What Penelope sees when she enters the great halls of her home is a stranger who has been mistreated by her suitors. These men are jeering and throwing things at the beggar, and they have no idea that he is actually Odysseus. Worse still, Penelope is appalled to witness her son standing idly by and allowing all of this to happen. Of course, we as readers know that this is simply part of Odysseus and Telemachus' plan. Yet that doesn't make Penelope's words any less true.

→

The queen cannot believe that her son would do nothing to help someone suffering such abuse. She stands up to the suitors and condemns their actions, welcoming the supposed stranger to her hearth as is customary in Greek mythology. For Penelope it is the worst kind of travesty to stand by and let another be mistreated when you could intercede.

Penelope may be a queen but as a woman in ancient Greece she certainly weilds less power than the men around her, but none of this holds her back. She knows the suitors outnumber her and her son, yet in her eyes this is no excuse to ignore an injustice when she sees one. It doesn't matter whether the man the suitors are insulting is a king or a humble beggar.

This sense of justice has always struck me as particularly admirable in Penelope. To strive to defend others against injustice is an incredible thing to do. Today, this might look like turning up to support a cause impacting people other than yourself, or saying something when you hear someone wielding their words with cruelty. As I'm sure Penelope would remind you, there are endless ways to show up for others.

It is the worst kind of travesty
to stand by and let another
be mistreated when you
could intercede.

"So these men urge on my marriage, and I wind a skein of wiles. First some god breathed the thought in my heart to set up a great web in my halls and fall to weaving a robe—fine of thread was the web and very wide; and I at once spoke among them:

'Young men, my suitors, since noble Odysseus is dead, be patient, though eager for my marriage, until I finish this robe—I would not have my spinning come to nothing—a shroud for the hero Laertes against the time when the cruel fate of pitiless death shall strike him down; for fear anyone of the Achaean women in the land should cast blame upon me, if he were to lie without a shroud, who had won great possessions.'

So I spoke, and their proud hearts consented. Then day by day I would weave at the great web, but by night would unravel it, when I had had torches placed beside me. Thus for three years

I kept the Achaeans from knowing, and beguiled them; but when the fourth year came, as the seasons rolled on, as the months waned, and the many days were brought in their course, then it was that by the help of my maids, shameless creatures and reckless, they came upon me and caught me, and upbraided me loudly. So I finished the web against my will, perforce. And now I can neither escape the marriage nor find some other device, and my parents are pressing me to marry, and my son frets, while these men devour his livelihood, as he is well aware; for by now he is a man, and fully able to care for a household to which Zeus grants honor."

19.138–61

LESSON THIRTY

THINK OUTSIDE THE BOX

"So these men urge on my marriage,
and I wind a skein of wiles."

19.138–39

If there is one thing you're guaranteed in abundance throughout the *Odyssey*, it is characters who think outside the box. Homer's poem is a positive slew of cunning plans, one after another, and not just from Odysseus. One of the most iconic examples of creative thinking in the epic is his wife Penelope's plan to stall her suitors.

As you know by now, during her husband's absence, Penelope is inundated with prospective replacements, whether she wants one or not. As the pressure to choose one of the men mounts, however, Penelope has an idea. She goes to them and explains that it would be unforgivable for her to remarry before she has finished weaving a death shroud for Odysseus' ageing father, Laertes. Surely, leaving such a task incomplete would shame her and any future husband she might take. The suitors concede Penelope's point but insist that once she is finished, then she must finally choose one of them to wed, to which she agrees.

The thing is, Penelope has no intention of finishing the shroud. Each day she dedicates her waking hours to weaving fabric on her loom as her servants watch on. No one can deny that she is constantly at work, thus upholding her end of the

bargain. Except at night, Penelope returns to her station in secret and unravels what she has accomplished that day. Thus, the shroud is never finished.

Perhaps unsurprisingly, Penelope cannot keep up this ruse forever. After four long years her lie is exposed, and she is forced to complete her task. Yet for four whole years she managed to keep the suitors at bay, thanks to her innovative thinking.

Penelope's trick has now become quite well-known, held up as a brilliant example of cunning from a character who is not to be underestimated. Although you might not be able to pull the exact same trick yourself, that does not mean you cannot take a little inspiration from the queen of Ithaca. Like her husband, Penelope is thoughtful and creative. As she puts it, she wound "a skein of wiles" when she did the unexpected.

The next time you're stuck on a project or feel like you're not getting any further forward with a goal you've set yourself, you might want to try Penelope's way of thinking, and look at the problem from another angle. Can you think outside the box to find your way around an obstacle? Penelope's plot is audacious and subverts what her suitors and the people around her would expect.

Sometimes overcoming our difficulties might just mean trying something different, perhaps even something Homeric.

Like her husband, Penelope is thoughtful and creative.

LESSON THIRTY-ONE

VALUE YOUR REST

"But let sleep now come over you.
There is weariness also in keeping wakeful
watch the whole night through; and you
are about to come out of your troubles."

20.51–54

Never underestimate the importance of a good night's sleep. This may be a simple lesson but it is no less integral to the heroic journey. Thanks to the invention of the cinematic montage, it might be easy to convince yourself that all it takes to defeat your enemy and win the war is to put yourself through a grueling series of physical exercises until you're carrying the weight of entire planets on your shoulders. This is an image that quickly translates to never stepping away from your desk or working long into the night when your battles look like paperwork or deadlines.

Yet there are countless moments in the *Odyssey* when Odysseus and the other characters must pause and, quite literally, take a nap—though occasionally it takes the gods themselves to slow them down. In Book Twenty, Odysseus is determined to push through his exhaustion and take back his home the moment he arrives on Ithaca. Athena, however, forces him to stop, going as far as to call him an "obstinate one" when he looks set on staying awake. Athena reminds Odysseus that refusing to sleep won't make the following day come any sooner. He will simply be more exhausted and less able to face the fight that comes.

→

Refusing to sleep won't
make the following day
come any sooner.

Now, none of this is to say that the *Odyssey* advocates abandoning all your other goals for comfortable pillows; that would hardly fit with the many lessons we've discussed so far. At one point the wise swineherd Eumaeus even warns that "there is weariness even in too much sleep." Yet, he adds: "As for the rest of you, if any man's heart and spirit bid him, let him go outside and sleep, and at daybreak let him eat, and follow our master's swine." (15.394–97)

So, perhaps the advice we should take away from both Athena and Eumaeus is to listen to your body. Don't overdo it. Rest is restorative. Because both character's words are applicable beyond the realms of Greek mythology. It's not just Homeric heroes who need to slow down once in a while; this advice also applies to you (and me).

There is nothing innately impressive or wise about pushing yourself beyond your limits, punishing your body, and denying yourself rest. It might even be time to put down this book and turn the light off for today ... It is more important that you learn to recognize when it is time to carry on and when it is time to lay your head down for the night.

PENELOPE

In many ways Penelope *is* the *Odyssey*. Throughout the epic Odysseus' return to Ithaca is unequivocally framed as a return to Penelope. She is his motivation. She is also the subject of much of the poem's narrative.

The daughter of the Spartan king Icarius and a nymph Asterodia, Penelope becomes the queen of Ithaca through marriage. We never hear much about her early years. It is only when she is given to Odysseus as a wife through the machinations of her uncle Tyndareus that she takes on a central role in Greek mythology. According to most accounts, she and her husband had only one child together—Odysseus' heir Telemachus.

Although like many mythological (and historical marriages) theirs was a strategic alliance, it is made very evident throughout the *Odyssey* that there is genuine love and affection between the two of them. By all accounts they are the perfect match. Do you think Odysseus intelligent? Meet Penelope: cunning, adaptable, patient, thoughtful, confident, discerning. Anything Odysseus is, so is she. And we see this demonstrated time and time again throughout the *Odyssey*.

When the noblemen of Ithaca come to claim Penelope as their bride in Odysseus' absence, she comes up with a plan to forestall them. It is a plan that Homer thought impressive enough to recount on three separate occasions. In Books Two,

→

[Odysseus] wept, holding in his arms his beloved true-hearted wife. And welcome as is the sight of land to men that swim, whose well-built ship Poseidon smashes on the sea as it is driven on by the wind and the swollen waves, and but few have made their escape from the gray sea to the shore by swimming, and thickly are their bodies crusted with brine, and gladly have they set foot on the land and escaped from their evil case; so welcome to her was her husband, as she gazed upon him, and from his neck still did not loosen her white arms at all. 23.231–40

Nineteen, and Twenty-four we hear of how Penelope informed the suitors that she could only take a new husband once she had finished weaving her father-in-law Laertes' death shroud. Note: Laertes was not yet dead; she was simply getting a head start on her marital duties.

The suitors accept her reasoning and agree to wait until she has finished her work. So, every day Penelope can be observed weaving a magnificent cloth on her loom and the suitors are satisfied. Except, unbeknownst to them, Penelope spends every night unraveling what she has accomplished the previous day. In this way the shroud remains unfinished for many years.

It is only when one of Penelope's maids reveals the queen's trick to the suitors that she is discovered. Otherwise, she could perhaps have gone on forever without any of the suitors catching on. Truly, they are depicted as clever Odysseus' opposites in every way. Even though she is eventually thwarted, let us not underplay the significance of Penelope's plan. How different would things have been had she not managed to keep the suitors waiting as long she did.

Penelope is often praised for her patience and loyalty, two qualities which might be summarized as commitment. The queen doesn't just demonstrate her commitment to Odysseus but to her laborious and time-consuming plan. Throughout the *Odyssey* her dedication to both people and tasks is exemplary.

For all her loyalty, meanwhile, Penelope could never be described as naive. Quite the opposite: she is both observant and discerning. One much-debated point regarding the *Odyssey* is whether Penelope recognizes Odysseus when he is disguised as a beggar. If she does, she never states it outright. Yet she comments to other characters that his feet and hands resemble her husband's.

But if Penelope recognizes Odysseus, why does she test him? When the suitors are dead and his identity is revealed, she refuses to accept Eurycleia's assurances that this is indeed her husband returned to her. If this seems strange, you must remember that Penelope has not seen her husband in twenty years; a period during which they have both aged and changed.

So, Penelope tests him. For she is nothing if not discerning. She asks Eurycleia to have their marital bed brought to the main hall, so that they might rest—a feat that only she and Odysseus know is impossible. When the hero shows his horror that the bed he carved from a still-living tree has been moved—in other words, cut down—Penelope is finally sure that he is indeed her husband. In the event Penelope *did* recognize Odysseus, this straightforward identity test leaves the reader with more questions than answers. Is it Penelope's attempt to be reunited with Odysseus on her own terms? Homer leaves it open to interpretation.

I think it's easy to be fooled by the memory of loyal, steadfast Penelope, and think of her as inexperienced and timid. Yet her confidence and cunning throughout the epic show her to be anything but. Penelope is patient, but she is not inactive. Nor should we allow our admiration for one person (like Odysseus) to overshadow another (like Penelope). She is her husband's equal.

So, while I think there is a lot we can learn from Penelope, some of which I've covered elsewhere in this volume, I think the lesson best exemplified by her character in the *Odyssey* is that you should never underestimate the quiet ones.

In many ways Penelope is the Odyssey. *Throughout the epic Odysseus' return to Ithaca is unequivocally framed as a return to Penelope. She is his motivation. She is also the subject of much of the poem's narrative.*

LESSON THIRTY-TWO

PICK YOURSELF BACK UP

Reaching up from here [Penelope] took from its peg the bow, together with the bright case which surrounded it. And there she sat down and laid the case upon her knees and wept aloud, and took out the bow of her husband. But when she had had her fill of weeping and crying, she went her way to the hall, to the company of the lordly suitors, bearing in her hands the back-bent bow and the quiver that held the arrows, and many arrows were in it, loaded with groanings.

21.51–60

As we approach the final hours of Homer's *Odyssey*, the time comes for Penelope to ready her husband's famous bow and arrow. Inspired by Athena, the queen has decided to initiate a contest between the suitors. Whichever suitor manages to string and fire Odysseus' bow is the one she will marry.

Before you scoff at Penelope's challenge, I must tell you that this is no ordinary bow. It was a gift to Odysseus from the Oechalian prince Iphitus as a mark of friendship when he was a youth. Its construction was infamously rigid, and as far as anyone knows Odysseus is the only one who can wield it.

Still, Penelope struggles with her plan; it is not an easy decision. The possibility that she might be forced to marry a man other than her husband, should he be able to string the bow, distresses her. She is also troubled by the fact that the contest itself might result in violence among the suitors and the others in her home—of whom the disguised Odysseus is one, whether she is aware of this or not. This is why she weeps.

→

In the end, however, Penelope must wipe away her tears and carry through her plan. She has overheard the suitors plotting and knows that if she does not bring their stay to an end, it will be her son who dies. It is no doubt a burden to make such a choice, but it is the only way to stop the suitors from murdering her son. Thus, Penelope sets in motion the *Odyssey*'s "final showdown."

As we have already seen, there is nothing shameful about sadness in the *Odyssey*. Emotions are a healthy and normal part of life; turmoil and grief are no exceptions. Homer in no way criticizes Penelope for her tears. What the poem recognizes is that there are times when we cannot wallow, when we must pick ourselves up, when we have "had our fill" of crying, and take steps to changing our circumstances. This is what Penelope does when she boldly approaches the suitors, and what we can all do by boldly approaching life, even when things get tough.

Penelope must wipe away
her tears and carry
through her plan.

HERMES

When you picture the god Hermes you probably envision a young man, lithe and clean-shaven, a broad-brimmed helmet atop his head, and winged sandals strapped to his feet. At least this is how he appears in most of his ancient depictions. The divine messenger whose unnatural speed makes him perfectly placed to dart between Olympus and Earth, carrying the words of the gods to mortals. Don't let his image fool you, though; Hermes was no youthful lackey. He was an incredibly powerful god in his own right.

One of the twelve Olympians, according to the *Homeric Hymn to Hermes*, Hermes was the son of Zeus and a nymph named Maia. It should be noted here that not all of Zeus' children received a place among the Olympians. No, Hermes was special. Within hours of his birth, while his mother slept, he had grown big enough to crawl. He then proceeded to journey all the way to Thessaly where he invented a musical instrument known as the lyre. Of course, this was long before the events of Homer's *Odyssey*, but with such an impressive start in life it was perhaps inevitable that he would play an important role in Odysseus' story.

Perhaps it is also unsurprising then that Hermes is the god of travelers, a role that is particularly appropriate in the *Odyssey* and its series of journeys. Whether it is to the Underworld or the next island over, Hermes serves as a guide and companion throughout the poem. He isn't always there, but he manages to turn up exactly when he is needed; an excellent reminder that help can occasionally come from places unexpected and unforeseen.

→

Cyllenian Hermes was calling forth the ghosts of the suitors. He held in his hands his wand, a beautiful wand of gold, with which he lulls to sleep the eyes of whom he will, while others again he wakens out of slumber as well; with this wand he roused and led the ghosts, and they followed [crying] ... and Hermes, the Helper, led them down the dank ways. 24.1–10

In many ways Hermes frames the entire narrative of the *Odyssey*. First when he instructs Calypso to send Odysseus on his way, as it is time the hero returned home, kickstarting Odysseus' new adventure. We encounter him for a second time toward the middle of the poem when he appears to Odysseus on Aeaea. Hermes warns the hero of the goddess Circe and gives him the tools he needs to survive their encounter unscathed. Then, in the final book of the poem, Hermes travels to Ithaca to guide the souls of the now dead suitors to the Underworld. He is there at the beginning and he is there at the end.

Through these three feats we witness the breadth of Hermes' powers. He is both intermediary and mediator. He is a messenger but also a companion. He is a guide as well as an advisor. Do these qualities remind you of anyone in your own life? How could you call on them for support when you need it?

All that's really missing from the character of Hermes in the *Odyssey* is the trickster persona we see elsewhere in Greek mythology (for example, when he steals the sacred cattle of Apollo, just for fun, then ensures they can't be found by enchanting the cows to walk backward). Rather than causing chaos for Odysseus, however, Homer's Hermes is a good luck charm. Literally Eriounes or "luck bringer" in the *Iliad*; an epithet that also fits Hermes' role in the *Odyssey*.

In some ways Hermes reminds me of that friend who you may not see all that often—perhaps due to distance or conflicting schedules—but who you know will always be there when you need them most, and vice versa. The knowledge that there's someone there you can call on if you need to, even if they're not right there all the time, can be a great source of comfort and security. Perhaps Hermes can even inspire you to channel some of this energy yourself. Show up for others when times are tough; be a companion who can navigate difficulties and be by their side. For, with friends like Hermes, it is impossible to be truly lost.

Hermes serves
as a guide
and companion
throughout
the poem.

LESSON THIRTY-THREE

GIVE THANKS

Then his father answered him, weeping: "Stranger, know that you have come to the country of which you ask, but wanton and reckless men now possess it. And all in vain did you bestow those gifts, the countless gifts you gave. For if you had found him [Odysseus] still alive in the land of Ithaca, then he would have sent you on your way with ample requital of gifts and good entertainment; for that is the due of him who begins the kindness."

24.280–85

Even in the final moments of Homer's *Odyssey*, there remains time for one final grand reveal. Odysseus, now restored to his former glory, pays a visit to his father Laertes. Blinded by age and grief, however, the older man fails to recognize his son. Thus, Odysseus decides to take on the guise of a travel-weary stranger one last time; perhaps reasoning that it is better to reveal himself slowly than give his elderly father too much of a shock.

As his invented persona, Odysseus explains to Laertes that he has come from far away to visit a brave hero named Odysseus, who he once hosted in his own palace years ago. Of course, Laertes still believes his son to be dead. He informs the stranger of this but assures him that should he have been here Odysseus would have welcomed him with countless gifts—a thank you for the kindness this stranger once showed him.

This last point Laertes is particularly emphatic about. He praises the son he believes he has lost for his capacity for gratitude. This quality is one that is integral to Odysseus' image, not just as a king, but as an honorable person. And though he is spoken of as if he is not present in this scene, we have seen Odysseus express thanks numerous times throughout the epic already.

→

In contrast with Odysseus, the suitor Antinous is reprimanded by Penelope for his own ingratitude. "Antinous," she addresses him, "full of violence, [and] deviser of evil!" (16.418) For, many years before, the suitor's father came to their home as a fugitive. Rather than turn him away, Odysseus defended him against those who threatened him. Antinous meanwhile returns to the same household that protected his father and bleeds it dry.

In Homer's *Odyssey*, showing others appreciation and recognizing when someone has done you a kindness is as admirable as any prowess with a weapon. Expressions of gratitude differentiate the heroic characters from the "villains."

No matter how big or small, being able to express gratitude is as much an admirable quality as it was three millennia ago. This can look like repaying someone else's generosity with a bed to sleep in or a home-cooked meal, as Laertes suggests in the *Odyssey*. But it can also be a simple verbalization of your appreciation, an acknowledgment of someone else's actions. In other words: a thank you. Never underestimate the power of a sincere expression of thanks.

Showing others appreciation and recognizing when someone has done you a kindness is as admirable as any prowess with a weapon.

Then he prayed to the daughter of great Zeus, and instantly raised aloft his long spear, and hurled it, and struck Eupeithes through the helmet with cheek-piece of bronze. This did not ward off the spear, but the bronze passed through, and he fell with a thud, and his armor clanged about him. Then on the foremost fighters fell Odysseus and his glorious son and thrust at them with swords and double-edged spears. And now they would have killed them all, and cut them off from returning, had not Athene, daughter of Zeus, who bears the aegis, shouted aloud, and held back all the fighters, saying:

"Cease from painful war, men of Ithaca, so that without bloodshed you may speedily be parted."

So spoke Athene, and pale fear seized them. Then in their terror the arms flew from their hands and fell one and all to the ground, as the goddess uttered her voice, and they turned toward the city, eager to save their lives.

Terribly then shouted the much-enduring, noble Odysseus, and gathering himself together he swooped upon them like an eagle of lofty flight, and at that moment the son of Cronus let go a flaming thunderbolt, and down it fell before the flashing-eyed daughter of the mighty sire. Then flashing-eyed Athene spoke to Odysseus saying:

"Son of Laertes, sprung from Zeus, Odysseus of many devices, hold your hand, and stop the strife of war, common to all, for fear Zeus, son of Cronus, whose voice is borne afar, may perhaps become angry with you."

So spoke Athene, and he obeyed, and was glad at heart. Then for the future a solemn truce between the two sides was made by Pallas Athene, daughter of Zeus, who bears the aegis, in the likeness of Mentor both in form and in voice.

24.520–48

LESSON THIRTY-FOUR

NO GOOD COMES OF ENDLESS FIGHTING

Athene, daughter of Zeus, who bears the aegis,
shouted aloud, and held back all the fighters, saying:
"Cease from painful war, men of Ithaca."

24.530–33

Though the events of the *Odyssey* take place a decade after the Trojan War, the conflict is as much a character in the *Odyssey* as any of the men or women who fill the epic. This is a poem defined by war. Rather than celebrate the Greek victory against the Trojans, though, the *Odyssey* repeatedly asks both its characters and readers to consider the value of such devastating hostilities.

What, if anything, is the point? And when must the fighting come to an end?

It is not insignificant that these questions are asked by the goddess of war herself. Though Athena guides Odysseus' hand as he slays his foe, she is also the one who recognizes when the fighting must end. I don't know that I would be so bold as to call the *Odyssey* an anti-war poem, but it is impossible to escape the fact that it largely focuses on the difficult aftermath of conflict: loss.

Though the *Odyssey* tells the story of the mythological past, one distant even to the ancient Greeks, these questions remain timeless. As modern readers there are also many things we might take away from this particular theme.

→

On a grand scale there are parallels to be drawn between the Trojan War and conflict in the contemporary world. Though our technology is different, we do not live in a world of peace any more than the ancient Greeks. For all we are sold a version of war as righteous and valiant, is the aftermath worth it? The loss of innocent lives, the destruction of homes, and trauma left untreated for both soldiers and civilians.

On a smaller scale, it is important to recognize when the conflicts we encounter in everyday life are getting us nowhere; to learn when to lay down our figurative arms and make the choice to move on.

Simply put, we must ask ourselves how the energy and resources that have so far fed violence might instead be used to create something better. This is the note the *Odyssey* ends on. The time for fighting, for war, is over. It is time for Odysseus to fulfill his obligations as ruler of Ithaca. It is time to rebuild and recover. It is time for peace.

The *Odyssey* largely focuses on the difficult aftermath of conflict: loss.

ITHACA
Coming Home

Despite the modern adoption of the word "odyssey" to refer to a long journey, the journey in the *Odyssey* arguably plays second fiddle to a far more important theme, *nostos*; in other words, Odysseus' homecoming.

Perhaps it's unfair to dismiss the importance of Odysseus' journey. After all, *nostos* in Ancient Greek referred to a hero's return home after a period of travel, so the ideas are interconnected. And this doesn't simply mean coming back after an hour or two spent fetching groceries or visiting friends. The Homeric homecoming is something far grander.

The island of Ithaca is the central point of the entire *Odyssey*. It is both Odysseus' ultimate destination and the geographical location we as readers spend the most time. Not only do we often visit its shores to check in on Telemachus, Penelope, and the suitors during the poem, but the entirety of the final eleven books takes place there. That's right, almost half of the *Odyssey* takes place after the return to Ithaca. As I said, in many ways the homecoming supersedes the journey.

Ithaca, at least the Ithaca described in Homer's *Odyssey*, does not directly correspond to any modern location; not even the Ithaca located to the west of mainland Greece today.

→

"I am Odysseus, son of Laertes, known to all men for my stratagems, and my fame reaches the heavens. I dwell in clear-seen Ithaca; on it is a mountain, Neriton, covered with waving forests, conspicuous from afar; and round it lie many islands close by one another, Dulichium, and Same and wooded Zacynthus. Ithaca itself lies low in the sea, farthest of all toward the dark, but the others lie apart toward the dawn and the Sun—a rugged island, but a good nurse of young men; and for myself no other thing can I see sweeter than one's own land." 9.19–28

As a ruler, Odysseus is committed to both his land and his people.

The geography as described by Homer just doesn't match up, although maybe Homer just wasn't great at geography. Regardless, when we speak about Ithaca in relation to the epic, we are talking specifically about a mythological kingdom.

Odysseus' Ithaca is described as a "rugged" island near the Greek mainland, but which gets less sunlight than its neighbors. It is supposedly rather flat and pretty unimpressive when compared to richer kingdoms like Sparta and Mycenae, but none of this matters to Odysseus. Odysseus, son of Laertes, was raised on Ithaca as its future king from birth. As a ruler, he is committed to both his land and his people, and this is one of the reasons he is so desperate to return.

Another more personal motivation is that Ithaca is where Odysseus' family resides. His wife, his father, and his son; the son who will one day be his successor but whom he has been unable to raise in person due to the Trojan War. For Odysseus, Ithaca is more than a kingdom; it is his home. If it weren't for its hero's unyielding desire to be reunited with his family, the *Odyssey* would have been significantly shorter. He might even have accepted one of the multiple goddesses who offered him a life of immortality as their companion. But he doesn't.

I appreciate it is something of cliché to follow up this analysis with the saying, "Home is where the heart is," but occasionally these stock phrases do contain a grain of truth. The difference is that home does not have to be where we grew up. Penelope, for example, is not a native of Ithaca. Like Helen, she was originally from Sparta—a city-state hundreds of miles away. Ithaca only becomes her home through marriage, yet her distress at the prospect of leaving her husband's palace for another man is palpable throughout the *Odyssey*.

Ithaca is the heart of Homer's epic. The entire narrative centers and ends around this one, relatively unimpressive island, all because it matters so much to those who call it home. In this way, the *Odyssey* is a story not about the journey but the destination. The trials and tribulations faced by Odysseus are worthwhile because in the end he has his *nostos*, his homecoming. For us, meanwhile, we might remember this when times are tough, work is hard, or coming up with new ideas feels like pulling teeth. In the end, it will all be worth it.

AFTERWORD

I was given my first copy of the *Odyssey* by my dad when I started university many, many years ago. On the first page he left me a message that I've never shared with anyone, but I'd like to share now:

For my dearest Jean,
The Odyssey *is a journey to redemption, a journey*
we all have to make sometime.
I will always be with you,
Dad

What neither myself nor my dad realized then, was that when I was twenty-five he would pass away. Yet, he was right when he wrote the words: "I will always be with you." My dad is still with me, in the knowledge he shared with me, in the passions he encouraged in me, and in the lessons he taught me. This is the way in which I believe people and art live on. Through their impact. And this is the way in which the *Odyssey* lives on.

For my dad, it was a tale of redemption. For me, it's a story about family. For you, the emphasis might fall on courage or personal growth. There is no one way to read the *Odyssey* and as we have seen, there is no singular lesson to take from its pages. The *Odyssey* is a piece of art that has lived a million lives, each one as important as the next.

ABOUT THE AUTHOR & ILLUSTRATOR

DR. JEAN MENZIES is an award-winning author, ancient historian, and presenter. She has a PhD in classics from the University of Roehampton, where she has also taught ancient history. Her specialties are ancient Greek literature, law, and mythology, as well as the history of women in antiquity. Jean has written nonfiction for children and adults, including *Greek Myths*, *Goddesses and Heroines*, *All the Violet Tiaras*, *Aphrodisia*, and *Live Like a Goddess*. Her debut novel, meanwhile, was an adult reimagining of Arthurian legend titled *The Lady of the Lake*. She also edits and compiles the *Myths and Legends* series for Macmillan Collector's Library. You can find Jean making videos on literature, history, and mythology over on her long-running YouTube channel Jean's Thoughts.

www.jeanmenzies.com | Instagram, TikTok, and YouTube: @JeansThoughts

BÁRBARA MALAGOLI is a Brazilian illustrator and visual artist based in London, UK. She has worked with a range of clients, including Nike, Samsung, and L'Oreal, as well as with publishers and publications such as *The New York Times* and the *Washington Post*. Her work is distinctive for its vibrant textures, bold colors, and creative compositions.

www.barbaramalagoli.com | Instagram: @bmalagoli

FURTHER READING

If you'd like to learn more about Homer's *Odyssey* and the history behind it, then check out these fantastic books:

Secondary Scholarship

Cosmopoulos, Michael B. (2025), *The World of Homer: Archaeology, Social Memory, and the Emergence of Greek Epic Poetry*, Cambridge University Press.
Deacy, Susan (2025), *The Greek Gods and Their Worlds*, Ivy Press.
Fowler, Robert (2004), ed., *The Cambridge Companion to Homer*, Cambridge University Press.
Graziosi, Barbara (2019), *Homer: A Very Short Introduction*, Oxford University Press.
Hauser, Emily (2025), *Mythica: A New History of Homer's World, Through the Women Written Out of It*, Doubleday.
Kostas, Myrsiades (2019), *Reading Homer's Odyssey*, Bucknell University Press.
Leeming, David (2003), *From Olympus to Camelot: The World of European Mythology*, Oxford University Press.
Nicolson, Adam (2025), *The Mighty Dead: Why Homer Matters*, William Collins.
Schein, Seth L. (2020), ed., *Reading the Odyssey: Selected Interpretive Essays*, Princeton University Press.
Shelmerdine, Cynthia (2008), *The Cambridge Companion to the Aegean Bronze Age*, Cambridge University Press.
Stevenson, Erica (2026), *The Odyssey Effect: How Homer's Epic Shaped the World*, Epic Ink.

Ancient Texts and Translations

Ahl, Frederick (2008), tr., *Virgil's Aeneid*, Oxford World Classics.
Hard, Robin (2008), tr., *The Library of Greek Mythology*, Oxford World Classics.
Lattimore, Richard (2011), tr., *The Iliad of Homer*, University of Chicago Press.
Melville, A. D. (2008), tr., *Ovid's Metamorphoses*, Oxford World Classics.
Murray, A. T. (1919), tr., *Odyssey*, Harvard University Press.
Rieu, E. V. (1946), tr., *The Odyssey*, Penguin.
West, M. L. (2008), tr., *Hesiod's Theogony and Works and Days*, Oxford World Classics.
Wilson, Emily (2017), tr., *The Odyssey*, W. W. Norton & Company.

INDEX

This book is dedicated to my cats, Mulder and Scully, because if I'm going to write about Odysseus' pet then mine deserve a little mention as well. – Jean

First published in 2026
by Rizzoli Universe, a division
of Rizzoli International Publications

Rizzoli International Publications Inc
49 West 27th Street, New York, NY 10001

Rizzoli International Publications UK Ltd
Somerset House, West Wing, Strand, London,
WC2R 1LA

www.rizzoliusa.com

Publisher: Charles Miers
Associate Publisher: Tina Persaud
Commissioning Editor: Isabel Jessop
Senior Editor: Kristy Richardson
Illustrator: Bárbara Malagoli
Designer: Sarah Pyke
Production Manager: Michelle Wells

A CIP catalogue record for this book is available from the British Library.

ISBN 978-0-7893-4679-7

FSC www.fsc.org MIX Paper | Supporting responsible forestry FSC™ C005748

2026 / 1

Printed in China

The authorized representative in the EU for safety and compliance is Mondadori Libri S.p.A., via Gian Battista Vico 42, Milan, Italy, 20123, www.mondadori.it

Visit us online:
Instagram.com/RizzoliBooks
Facebook.com/RizzoliNewYork
Youtube.com/user/RizzoliNY